# EMPOWERING LEADERSHIP

**Developing Behaviors for Success**

ISBN: 978-0-8389-8657-8

Published by:
**American Association of School Librarians**
a division of the American Library Association
50 E. Huron St.
Chicago, Illinois 60611-2795

To order, call 800-545-2433, press 7
<www.alastore.ala.org/aasl>

# Acknowledgments

*AASL gratefully acknowledges the following:*

## Written by:

Ann M. Martin
Educational Specialist
Henrico County Public Schools, Virginia
<libraryann@comcast.net>

AASL Staff Liaison: Stephanie Book

*AASL Publications purchases fund advocacy, leadership, professional development, and standards and guidelines initiatives for school librarians nationally.*

# Table of Contents

# Introduction

Leadership became the next great frontier for school librarians' professional growth with the emergence of two important documents from the American Association of School Librarians (AASL): *Standards for the 21st-Century Learner* and *Empowering Learners: Guidelines for School Library Programs*. The secret to successful school library programs seemed to be in how librarians seized leadership opportunities for guiding initiatives and learning in the school community. School librarians wanted to know how to insert leadership into their already-packed days. They found that this additional role was intangible and so significant that it was hard to grasp. In fact, leadership characteristics are both observable and vague.

So how do school librarians develop a set of leadership skills that inspires stakeholders' buy-in for the school library program and leads to success in meeting goals? Throughout the history of school libraries many exemplary leaders have furthered the profession and supported students' success. Some leaders provided a national vision, some regional insight, some local guidance, and many others were models at the building level. Yet in order for librarians as a group to become great leaders they must discover the leaders inside themselves.

Leadership has visible and invisible attributes. Many books define the observable aspects of leadership, but *Empowering Leadership: Developing Behaviors for Success* unveils the hidden qualities that create confident, successful leaders. Each of the five sections explains how leadership applies to school librarians in the way they manage people, develop dispositions, communicate, accept responsibility, and reflect on their own skills as leaders. Essential questions provide a framework for each chapter. School librarians can use these questions to pre-assess their own leadership actions and beliefs. Within the text librarians will recognize the hidden leadership opportunities in daily tasks that are central to the profession. At the end of each chapter are suggestions for librarians to put into practice. These tips are concrete actions and suggestions for ways librarians can demonstrate leadership. Every librarian has inherent leadership abilities; this book provides the means to consciously develop qualities that create great leaders.

Reading this book takes the mystery out of leadership by illustrating the visible and invisible components of leadership. Reflective strategies in the text and tips at the end of each chapter will bring school librarians to their next level in leadership development. Librarians become great leaders when they create relevance for the school library program as the future unfolds. As leaders they promote library best practices, are proactive, and apply professional skills, dispositions, responsibilities, and assessment in guiding library programs. *Empowering Leadership: Developing Behaviors for Success*, offers lessons and examples to improve the leader within and encourage development of each librarian's unique leadership style. Librarians will lead by example, making visible the very leadership concepts and qualities that seem so elusive and difficult to understand.

# Section 1

# What Do You Say to *That?*

**PEOPLE**

"What do you say to *that?*" came at the end of an exchange between a young child and his mother. Leaders contemplate answering the same question when communicating with colleagues and other stakeholders. In this instance a child was playing, and his mother needed him to take a break to celebrate his grandfather's birthday. The child was having too much fun, and he did not want to stop playing. One excuse after another was forthcoming. Finally, the mother said, "Graydon, your grandfather is the most important person in this world; get in here right now." Graydon immediately replied, "So what about God?" His mother just smiled and said, "What do you say to *that?*"

Without people, leaders and leadership is meaningless. An organization is composed of many personalities with diverse needs. It is leadership of people that creates success or destroys an organization. A leader knows what to say to facilitate positive action. Clearly, knowing what is important to people and motivates their responses into meaningful solutions is a role of a leader.

# Chapter 1

# Knowing Your Customers

**Leadership questions related to knowing your customers are:**

▶ Is what is being discussed in the school hallways the same as what is being discussed in the library office?

▶ How do leaders create change?

▶ How do people in an organization impact communication style?

A scholarship applicant recently mentioned that by shelving books she discovered titles she would never have read. Hidden on the shelves, books tend to recede in importance. Every librarian knows that creating book displays encourages interest and increases awareness of books by otherwise forgotten authors. When Margot Livesey's book *The Flight of Gemma Harvey* created renewed interest in the classic *Jane Eyre*, librarians marketed both. Putting both books in front of customers drew attention to the similarities of the stories, yet the unique qualities of the characters and the important differences in plot began discussions among readers. Connecting the two books benefited readers and library programs.

Just as librarians connect readers to books, leaders connect people in an organization to less tangible and visible goals. To achieve this connection, leaders must get out from behind the desk to gain knowledge of the story, characters, and key issues important to people in the organization. Though many important activities must be done in the leader's office, the real story lies with the people whose work contributes to the organization. Hidden back in the departments are needs, questions, and concerns. Some of these issues will never be known outside the departments, much less reach the leader's office. For a school librarian this reality means getting out and meeting formally and informally with administrators, teachers, students, parents, and community members. Creating a communication network is essential for the library leader. Conversation and openness make the school librarian aware of underlying needs of teachers and students. Awareness of needs and understanding people in the school community allow the school librarian to analyze concerns and offer library solutions whenever and wherever appropriate.

## REAL-LIFE EXAMPLE

Recently Talitha Matlin and Amy Jankowski, librarians for San Diego Zoo Global (SDZG) collected data on the use of the library throughout the organization. After tracking reference interactions and library traffic for three months, the data confirmed anecdotal evidence that suggested those employees in closer proximity to the library used the library more. Among the group not using library resources on a regular basis were zookeepers and horticulturists who would need to travel forty-five minutes to access the library. Talitha and Amy found that since patrons are dispersed over a large geographical area, the users were not receiving equal access to library resources. Inspired by San Diego Zoo Global's Vision "to become a world leader in connecting people to wildlife and conservation," the librarians pursued alternatives so that all employees would have access to "high-quality information sources they could use to optimize their performance" (Jankowski and Matlin 2012). Their solution was to reach out to users through a multi-pronged approach. The librarians developed a mobile library that was brought to employees' break areas during lunch hours. This mobile collection included a variety of resources that targeted horticulturists' and zookeepers' needs. The librarians brought newsletters, new materials, and sample factsheets related to new exhibits. They also gave employees an opportunity to register to receive updates and news from the library. Their advocacy campaign also included providing bookmarks listing basic resources and contact information. These librarians advertised their print and digital resources as well as their expertise in providing research assistance. Using e-mail and daily e-newsletters, they advertised mobile hours, upcoming visits, and library outreach events.

Talitha and Amy's efforts resulted in a 184 percent increase in circulation over a six-month period. Their reference interactions increased by 26.5 percent during weeks with outreach. Making personal contact and going to patrons increased usage even during weeks when the mobile library was not able to visit the zookeepers and horticulturists. Those weeks without mobile library outreach gave rise to a 5.8 percent increase. Contact with the users broadened the library base, increased communication, and provided opportunities for employees to better perform their jobs (Jankowski and Matlin 2012).

This outreach also provided insight about employees' needs because, by circulating among users, Talitha and Amy gained a better understanding of the people who work for San Diego Zoo Global. Lee G. Bolman and Terrence E. Deal, in their book *Reframing Organizations: Artistry, Choice, and Leadership*, explained that answers require a thoughtful knowledge of people and their interdependent relationship with the organization (2008). For leaders to fully grasp the employee-organization relationship they must be visible, gather perspectives, and share information. For example, Talitha and Amy learned that some employees never visit the break room at lunch. Other employees work in offsite offices and field stations. The data from Talitha and Amy's project provide compelling evidence of the difference personal contact makes on a library program. Research and communication provide leaders with an understanding of how to support employees while remaining focused on goals of the organization. Random and frequent visits with those in the field result in discussions and create opportunities for understanding. Like Talitha and Amy, an effective leader must be willing to go to the people, ask questions, observe the work environment, and listen.

So, the San Diego Zoo Global study provides evidence that getting out from behind the desk and into the field drives meaningful change. Effective leaders purposely schedule time to pull together perspectives from people in the organization. Likewise, school librarians must deliberately cultivate confidence in their ability to guide educational change rather than react to decisions that are made. A large part of leadership is being on the front side of decisions, guiding the dialog, and creating solutions to educational problems that impact the school library program. One way to do that is to know what is important to decision makers, and to staff and students in the school.

## APPLYING SKILLS LIBRARIANS ALREADY HAVE

The best method for finding out what people need is to search for pertinent accurate information. Locating and using information is a foundational skill essential to our profession. Librarians recognize when information is needed and then locate, evaluate, and use the research data. Leadership of the school library program benefits from librarians using information-literacy skills when seeking and analyzing the school environment. To collect data about initiatives, librarians will not only seek information inside the walls of the school, they will also interact with people who are part of the school community but outside the school walls. Just as school librarians strive to develop learners who are independent seekers of information, librarians must consider the very same information-literacy skill to be a leadership tool.

School librarians teach learners that they must define the problem and/ or create an essential question when they begin information-seeking. Librarians who are knowledgeable of the work environment define problems that will surface from new initiatives, agendas, and mandates. Next, they go into the school halls and departments to collect information. Leaders determine where to begin their information-seeking by asking the essential question, "Who are the key stakeholders in this initiative?" Once a complete list of people has been identified, the librarians formally and informally meet with each stakeholder. These people resources provide answers to issues related to proposals because dialog encourages individuals to explain their understanding and needs as they relate to initiatives.

Just as students take notes, leaders also must keep a log of information and insights gained from conversations. Good leaders consciously listen and observe body language when acquiring relevant information. Because fear creates a gap between implementation and success, leaders also know to note if colleagues express fears about changes. This gap provides a leadership opportunity for librarians to create school library program solutions. Change in the library program that provides support for organizational goals is welcomed instead of resisted because users' needs are answered.

## FOCUS ON STAKEHOLDERS' CONCERNS

Leaders know that sharing information is critical to ensuring effective and efficient fulfillment of goals and objectives. The first rule when communicating change is to know your audience. Recently a state university Board of Visitors forced the president to resign. This action resulted in major demonstrations and petitions signaling a lack of confidence in the Board. A reporter stated that communication of information was "opaque." It was also mishandled. One explanation for the mismanagement was that the rector, vice rector, and another member of the Board of Visitors were successful in real estate, construction, and investing. The reporter noted that they saw an opportunity to use their business knowledge in their role overseeing the university. The author of the commentary stated that treating universities like a business was a mistake (Keep 2012). He explains that universities have some of the same problems as businesses such as allocating budgets and long-term market values. What he also confirms is that qualities that educators value most are long-term goals as opposed to short-term fixes. The firing of the university president may have been a good financial decision but it was abrupt and clouded with back room finagling. Unfortunately, these Board members did not know their customers. They used business terminology and practices to justify the release of the president. One Board member used the business term "'strategic dynamism' to describe the ever-reactive leadership style he prefers, which is opposed to the older, more static 'strategic planning' style employed by" the university president (Keep 2012). The Board of Visitors announced the decision excluding the faculty, students, and most alumni. The decision lacked insight into the long-term values and qualities that educator's value. Successful leaders consider with whom information is being shared and clearly express the information's relevance to customers. After twenty days of unrest, which included resignations of members of the Board of Visitors, campus protests, and alumni weighing in from across the state and the nation, the university president was reinstated (Winter 2012). In this circumstance the university's customers were unprepared for the information, and the Board of Visitors misread their role when communicating information.

This is an example of the problems that may arise when communication does not connect with the audience.

When conveying information in the school setting, librarians need to understand the communications structure of the school. Making sure that the person in charge knows about any new library program idea is essential for support. Communicating ideas to administration serves as an advocacy tool and often functions as a feasibility check on how the new facet of the program is perceived.

A useful method for presenting ideas to busy administrators is to create a one-page synopsis of the goal with objectives and an action-plan timeline. After the administration approves the plan, librarians use the structural procedures in the school to share the plan with those it will impact. Whether the school has a departmental team or grade-level structure, information must be explained to the primary user-group first. Then sharing information with others in the school community follows.

A leader knows the structural processes in the organization and uses this knowledge to advantage. Typically, the procedures in place are designed to bring about buy-in from one segment of the organization at a time. The school librarian who knows which stakeholders should be approached first, recognizes what communication format is most acceptable, and shows program relevance will achieve acceptance of the information shared.

Leaders understand that to gain respect for a vibrant school library program their customers' needs must be met. This focus on customers is not about leaders providing what they think customers want but about having an honest dialog in which leaders seek clarity and deep understanding of customer needs and requests. Leaders acquire this deep understanding by immersing themselves into the formal and informal culture of the organization; this immersion allows leaders to know what the people who influence workplace dynamics require. Librarians who embrace people in the organization initiate a consistent flow of information. This customer-driven information provides problem-solving opportunities for the librarian. Although leaders prefer to create solutions before problems become big, they also realize that sharing information is critical to resolving issues.

## LEADERSHIP TIPS RELATED TO KNOWING YOUR CUSTOMERS

► Connect to the people in the organization by going to them.

► Find the needs, questions, and concerns hidden in the curriculum departments and grade-level classrooms.

► Create a communication network—it is essential.

► View information literacy as a leadership tool.

► Create opportunities for understanding by making random and frequent visits with those in the school.

► Be willing to listen.

► Observe body language to fully gather relevant information.

► Consider who the information is being shared with and clearly express the information's relevance to that audience.

► Know the structural processes in the organization and use them to your advantage.

► Resolve issues by sharing information in a language and style that customers understand.

# Chapter 2

# Assessing and Approaching Power Brokers

**Leadership questions related to assessing power brokers and their concerns are:**

▶ What is important to power brokers?

▶ How can library initiatives be positioned to accomplish successful support?

▶ Would circumventing the decision-making process help or hinder initiatives?

Original paintings by local artists were displayed on the wall of a coffee shop. One artist was delighted—and a bit surprised—when his watercolor of a Japanese garden was the first painting in the group to sell. After all, it was winter, and the spring painting was anything but seasonal. Little did the artist know that the impetus for this purchase began months before when he was planning the work. When asked about his process, the artist explained that the hardest part of the painting process is picking a subject. Once a subject has been selected, a sketch that is an outline of the painting is created. Then the artist decides the sequence in which to paint the parts of the sketch to achieve a three-dimensional look when the painting has been completed. Extremely important are the patterns and the detail work, which make aspects of the painting more or less important to the eye of the viewer. The artist explained that before he is finished he solicits another opinion to see what might be missing from the painting or what portion of the scene needs touching up. And then when asked, "What sells a painting?" he replied that he intentionally markets the ones with visual appeal (Martin 2012).

So how does this story even remotely equate with leadership? Just as this artist had a plan and a process for his art, leaders also recognize the need for a plan and process when seeking buy-in for initiatives. As the painting develops through the artistic process, this artist takes deliberate steps, planning and assessing the work to reach the final objective. Leaders understand that gaining support for initiatives takes planning—and that this planning requires knowledge about the organization in which change will be made. Just as patterns emerge in an artist's work so are patterns evident in the school setting. Creating a sketch or an outline of the organization is important. This environmental sketch, just like the artist's painting, is only as clear as the details collected. So, in developing a summary of the school's organizational framework, analyze the power brokers and what influences their choices. Just as the artist prioritizes what should be painted and in what sequence, the leader sets priorities as well. Begin by assessing the patterns and processes used by power brokers to manage the school. Gaining knowledge about who influences management outcomes in the school reveals the organization's level of complexity.

## APPLYING SKILLS LIBRARIANS ALREADY HAVE

The leader who analyzes school decision makers by examining variables in the organization gains an understanding of the operational dynamics of the school (Bolman and Deal 2008). Librarians acquire materials and then catalog them for use. To do these tasks, they first determine what materials are available for purchase and then categorize them. School librarians can transfer this skill into acquiring information about power brokers in the school.

Documenting school dynamics not only identifies decision makers but also reveals who influences their actions. Leaders identify these important people and the range of their authority. For example, sometimes all requests must go through the principal of a school for approval, but, by observing school practices, librarians may note that an assistant principal has extensive influence over responses to requests. Leaders observe the school environment and identify people in positions of authority who are respected by the principal.

Once key decision makers and their trusted advisors are identified, leaders calculate the impact those people have on acceptance of library program initiatives. Prior to seeking approval from the principal, leaders will act on this information and make sure that key advisors support initiatives. Librarians who understand their schools' cultures and the concerns of power brokers will effectively move school library program proposals through schools' hierarchies. Effective leadership of school library programs results because these school librarians understand who is important to decisions and what influences those decisions.

Good military leaders must have good intelligence gathering, good planning, and good tactics to articulate and then achieve goals. School librarians need all these elements—and probably more—when assessing power brokers in their schools. Through their own intelligence-gathering, and analysis of power brokers' management styles and practices, librarians gain valuable insight into how power brokers operate. Gathering information about the school's operations will reveal the workings of a complex interdependent environment (Bolman and Deal 2008).

Of course, resources are finite. When one department gains, another typically loses resources, time, or funding. Conflict can be reduced by knowing who will react to initiatives and then forming a plan to address their concerns. Information about existing values, policies, procedures, and needs in the school clarifies the interconnected web-like influences impacting operation of the school. Showing interdependence among resources in the online catalog—a skill familiar to all school librarians—is similar to sorting information about the school culture and making relevant connections.

The revised cataloging standard known as *Resource Description and Access* (RDA) is the new standard designed for the digital world. It will allow bibliographic information in the catalog to evolve from flat, linear data to linked data expressing relationships between works, expressions, manifestations, and items (Morgan 2012). Using the principles of RDA, school librarians need to assess information about organizational practices to show relationships within the school. To understand how power brokers make choices, a school librarian must examine how policies affect decisions, which people contribute to acceptance or rejection of ideas, and whether the beliefs of the school's stakeholders will impact acceptance and implementation of a new idea. RDA protocols link data, thus connecting varied resources into a web-like arrangement. This linking expands the accessibility not only of the resources directly sought, but also of related resources (Morgan 2012).

Just as RDA enhances access and shows interconnectivity between bibliographic records, the school librarian who examines existing values, policies, procedures, and needs is increasing opportunities for positive decisions. The same analytical skills used to catalog materials can be transferred by the librarian to form a multidimensional overview of the school. Revealing the interdependent nature of the school structure enables leaders to successfully anticipate acceptance or rejection of ideas.

## USING ESTABLISHED PATTERNS AND FOCUSING ON STAKEHOLDERS' CONCERNS

Leaders know that obstacles surface when the decision makers and stakeholders are not informed about changes. Often, complications occur when changes are not explained in language decision makers and stakeholders understand. So, how do leaders communicate to manage or avoid bureaucratic obstacles? Avoiding bureaucratic obstacles is easy for leaders because they understand the way the organization works and use established patterns to push ideas through the system. Instead of letting the system run them, leaders manage the system. They know their customers, and they understand the processes for moving new ideas through the system. They avoid creating conflict by using the established protocol. In addition, they use communication to provide understanding and reinforce beliefs that are important to staff. They ensure that any new program idea is aligned with policy. Informing stakeholders in ways they are familiar with and using terminology they understand prevents misunderstanding and promotes buy-in.

When finding acceptance for a new program, following organizational best practices creates an opportunity for success. Begin with developing a concise outline for the project. This outline provides an overview of the goals, objectives, timeline, and expenses for the project. This outline is equivalent to the artist's sketch. And just as the artist prioritizes what to paint first, leaders decide who to approach and when to filter the idea through the organization. For example, if the project directly impacts certain departments in the school, then the librarian goes to the customers in those specific departments and asks them to review the plan.

Leaders take time to find answers to questions constituents may have and listen for concerns. Leaders maintain strict confidentiality when gathering data and input. Librarians who communicate clearly to stakeholders about the intent and benefits of a project create buy-in and squelch opposition. Seeking input from others and demonstrating respect for colleagues' opinions promote two-way understanding. Partnerships materialize as leaders value colleagues' points of view. In the end, these coalitions help move a project through the approval process.

Just as the artist asks for input and adds details to the painting, leaders revise initiatives incorporating new data and information obtained during the communication process. This process is like painting details on a canvas to emphasize important aspects and minimize nonessential pieces of the project (Martin 2012). Once the project outline has been vetted and revised, then school librarians should seek one more check from selected colleagues before taking it to the administration. The initiative should now have collegial support because end-user concerns and issues are addressed in the plan. In addition, a marketing strategy evolves that answers stakeholder concerns and issues. This marketing reflects how the initiative saves time, funds, and resources or has the potential to increase students' success. The new program initiative is now ready to be brought before the administration for approval.

Leaders have no more control over decision makers than an artist has over the purchaser of a painting. Or do they? Decision makers use repetitive practices when evaluating ideas. The questions they ask, the concerns they have, and the objectives they want to meet will follow a pattern. A leader anticipates these patterns but, more importantly, values knowing how these patterns have an impact on organizational decisions. As a result of their awareness, leaders know how to position requests in a way that gains acceptance.

Unconsciously librarians know how the school operates. Just as children know which parent to go to for approval, librarians know who the decision makers are in their schools. Effective school librarians observe and reflect on what is important to decision makers and position new initiatives in the context of school goals. Leaders understand what written and unwritten procedures are important to power brokers in their school. Challenging these procedures equates with failing to give users passwords to research databases. All the groundwork is completed, the databases are set up, but student research is unavailable because a critical component was not provided. Just as a password opens databases for users, processes and procedures provide access to decisions. The processes are set up by power brokers to assist them in decision making. These processes reflect what is important to power brokers when organizational changes are considered. Following standard operating procedures shows respect for the structures in place and gains support for initiatives. So, follow the schools operating guidelines when seeking approval.

Like artists, leaders must have a plan in place to gain acceptance of ideas. Leaders consciously assess organizational practices to determine what is important to power brokers. They understand the interrelated workings of the people in the organization. And, when initiating change, leaders use the structural procedures and seek advice from those who are respected by decision makers. Final acceptance results when the leader sells the project by intentionally appealing to the processes and beliefs valued by power brokers.

---

## LEADERSHIP TIPS RELATED TO ASSESSING POWER BROKERS' CONCERNS

▶ Recognize that gaining support for initiatives takes planning.

▶ Assess what influences power brokers.

▶ Know that change is an outcome of new ideas.

▶ Understand that roadblocks appear when any segment of the school community feels threatened.

▶ Remember that communication is essential to gain support for new ideas.

▶ Maintain strict confidentiality when gathering data and input.

▶ Find answers to questions and listen for concerns from colleagues.

▶ Establish coalitions to help move a project through the approval process.

▶ Follow written and unwritten procedures important to decision makers.

▶ Seize marketing opportunities that arise when a project fills an organizational need.

# Chapter 3

# Building Strong Partnerships

**Leadership questions related to building strong partnerships are:**

▶ What are mutually beneficial solutions?

▶ How does management of people relate to negotiation?

▶ Can unity be created from diverse opinions and perspectives?

Political elections can confuse the most intelligent citizen. Many candidates decide to run for an office, and each is quick to point out differences among their opponents. Each candidate's team of advisors researches opponents to expose conflicting details, and advertisements are created using sound bites that are turned into political philosophy. Weeks and months slip by until one candidate becomes the party's choice and then opposing candidates stand on stage together as a sign of unity. In the long run, it is mutually beneficial for the candidates to form partnerships. Individual agendas are filtered through a negotiation process as contenders resolve diverse opinions. The party platform unites all because candidates know the end result of working together means meeting the party's election goals.

Leaders seek solutions that are mutually beneficial. This means that leaders seek outcomes to benefit people's varied needs. When discussion and action plans focus diverse perspectives toward organizational goals, people unite to achieve success. In the school setting these partnerships are created when leaders understand colleagues and their needs. Solutions that are mutually beneficial to differing departments result in incremental gains for those departments.

## APPLYING SKILLS LIBRARIANS ALREADY HAVE

Librarians are trained to collaborate while seeking mutually beneficial solutions for student learning. The collaborative process provides insight to differing needs when working toward common instructional goals. Every day librarians collaborate to identify paths toward student success and then create those paths by constructing lesson plans, purchasing resources, and developing programs. This process is not new to school librarians because their library training includes practice in skilled collaboration.

One May, our principal came to a colleague and me (the two librarians in the school) and stated, "We are going to apply for National Blue Ribbon School recognition, and I want you to lead this project." Immediately, negative thoughts streamed through our minds. Really, it is May, and in six weeks school will end; summer vacation will kick in; and the application must be completed by the beginning of September. The details needed to pull off this project seemed impossible! Obviously, pleasing the principal would be beneficial, and if the school *did* receive the prestigious award, then it would bring honor to the students, teachers, administration, and the school. Therefore, we accepted leadership of the project.

Our plan was to form partnerships with staff members and collaborate on an action plan. We knew our colleagues well, and asked four teachers to help: people with excellent organizational skills, dedication to large projects, and overt support of the principal. The six-member team created a timeline by starting with the September due date and progressing backwards to May. The project was divided into four distinct segments. Each of the four teachers began pulling together a team to work on his or her segment. Based on the team's timeline, deadlines for each section's completion were established. When the teacher leading part one finished, she passed the document to the leader of part two, and so on.

Meanwhile, the school librarians served as data gatherers, pumping research information to each section leader. The application was finished on time, and, remarkably, the school was awarded the Blue Ribbon designation by the United States Department of Education. The outcome was remarkable but not surprising. We, the librarians, knew our colleagues' strengths and understood that the school culture would support working toward a defined goal. As school librarians, we used our professional skill of collaboration to form a successful partnership among colleagues. Forming a team, we distributed the workload. This collaborative approach transformed a massive task into manageable units. As school librarians, my colleague and I showed leadership by completing a goal that was mutually beneficial to all.

## INVESTING IN RELATIONSHIPS

Negotiations were unnecessary in the example of the National Blue Ribbon School application project because everyone involved was united toward achieving the goal. But what happens when projects are proposed, and key people in the school are philosophically opposed to completing them? Often this opposition is because people believe that the project encroaches on their area.

Schools are political entities with finite resources. When a new program emerges, segments of the school community anticipate loss of time, funds, or resources (Bolman and Deal 2008). In situations like this leaders understand negotiation is needed because they expect concerns to emanate from fear of anticipated loss. Leaders brainstorm outcomes that move compromise forward. Sometimes this compromise means giving up specific proposals to gain important objectives. Successful negotiations are based on the concept that the parties involved must each contribute to the solution. In the school environment compromise is essential when multiple colleagues have differing opinions.

For negotiation strategies to be successful, investing time in developing people relationships and focusing attention on stakeholders' concerns is vital. Book challenges are instances where school librarians practice this diplomacy to ensure the gap between selection policy and society values is fairly explored.

## REAL-LIFE EXAMPLE

Recently a parent wanted a book taken off the school library's shelf because she felt the material was too mature for her first-grade student. Supposedly, her child had heard about a book that was a fifth-grade title. When the child went to the library he found the fifth-grade book on the shelf. Ironically, the student never checked the book out. The library assistant tracks students, and the school librarian, who was teaching a class, saw productive students at work in the library. Many checks and balances are used in this well-run library from sign-in and sign-out procedures to routine scanning of the library by the librarian and library assistant. If the child actually found the book, he would not have had a great deal of time to explore the contents. But the child went home and told his parents about the book. As a result, the parent checked the book out of the public library and read it cover to cover. Meanwhile, a teacher in the school was approached by the parent and ended up agreeing with the parent.

The school librarian was in a situation where she had to protect the integrity of the other teacher and uphold the selection policy, which is based on the American Library Association's Library Bill of Rights. The school librarian reached out to the parent to discuss the situation. Throughout the conversation this parent seemed immovable. She wanted the book taken off the shelf immediately. The parent made it clear that all her neighbors agreed with her and supported her concerns.

Consider how negotiations have a place here. The school librarian knew that the book was not going to be removed from the shelf without going through the instructional review process. Since the book had been purchased under selection-policy guidelines, was age-appropriate, and written on an upper-elementary student's reading level, the librarian was fairly sure that the review committee would retain the title. However, she knew that a community uprising over a book was not beneficial to the school's atmosphere as a community of learners and people who care about those learners.

When dialog is at a stalemate a leader will reflect back to analyze major issues that have been verbalized. This reflection is exactly what the librarian did. She knew that book challenges are the result of fears. In this case, the parent strongly felt that a child was confronted with issues before he was emotionally mature enough to understand information in the book. This fear was driving that parent's complaint. The student in this situation had questions and went to the parent for answers. Ideally, this behavior is what should happen. However, as a result, the parents felt obligated to make sure no other child is exposed to inappropriate materials.

The school librarian thought about possible solutions as she listened to the parent's comments. Politely, she allowed the parent to express her concerns fully. The librarian agreed that the book was neither appropriate for nor of interest to younger students, but the librarian emphasized that upper-elementary students needed to have choices on the library shelves to address their needs. The librarian wanted the book available for student use. The parent needed to be validated and be able to take a tangible outcome away from the situation. Then the librarian decided that the real issue in this situation was need for a discussion about student responsibility and vigilance by the library staff to follow monitoring procedures already in place. The book belonged on the shelf for upper-elementary students, yet a plan to ensure younger students stayed on task when in the library needed to be reviewed. The parent eventually agreed and together they settled on strategies to ensure students who came into this very active library to check out books remained on task. Shifting the parent's focus from book censorship to student responsibility created a win-win solution to the problem. The book remained on the shelf, and student guidance during checkout was reevaluated.

Listening for opportunities to resolve differences is what makes leaders successful negotiators. This librarian correctly identified the root of the problem and directed the parent to an appropriate resolution. She could have allowed the book to go through the review process, but the librarian realized that the process would keep the book on the shelf. The real problem was not the book, but the fact that the book landed in the hands of a student for whom it was not age-appropriate (Roberts 2012).

## BUILDING BRIDGES

Negotiation and compromise are tools school librarians can use to bring about effective resolutions to situations in which stakeholders have differing ideas. Every organization has divergent thinkers who skew acceptance of new ideas. These people verbalize concerns that require more research and frequently throw a monkey wrench into the progression of a project. So what does the good leader do with that situation?

Leaders are grateful for conflicting or opposing questions and comments. They accept diverse opinions and ideas into discussions because this acceptance fosters ownership for outcomes while preventing groupthink. Much has been written about groupthink, which means that all members of a team think alike to lessen conflict. Groupthink stalls creativity and innovation because it eliminates alternative ideas (Dictionary.com 2012). A confident leader takes all opinions and creates a bridge between ideas and visions for a proposed project.

By bridging ideas the leader creates unity. So, how do leaders achieve this outcome? They analyze and synthesize information. They document diverse opinions, research the ideas, and decide what part of the idea is useful to the project—in other words, exercise more of the skills librarians already have. School librarians work with every student, every teacher, every administrator, and every community member. Serving as librarian of a school presents multiple opportunities to hear differing opinions. Every day librarians encounter situations that demand cooperation. Some, such as lesson development, are routine. However, large projects, such as renovations or new library construction, require school librarians to unite diverse opinions.

## REAL-LIFE EXAMPLE

One example of this challenge was during renovation of a high school library. The architect introduced a beautiful design concept that was unrealistic for practical use. In this case, the librarians wanted to encourage functionality so they used the bridging technique to facilitate changes. To put more square footage into the front office, the design team wanted to take a large section from the side of the library. Initially, the librarians were devastated and wondered just how the smaller library could manage to hold multiple classes and activities.

Knowing that architects see space differently than educators, the librarians valued the architects' concept, compiled research on the major activities that take place in the library, and came back to the architects with detailed data and information. The librarians validated the beneficial concepts while providing evidence to adjust portions of the design that were problematic to the school library program. The architect now understood library activity and instructional goals. By extending the roof of the library at the opposite end of the room, the architect increased library space. This change supported the library program's need for space while dedicating vital square footage to the front office. Rather than folding to the architect's first proposal, the librarians took leadership of the situation in a rational, data-driven way. The additional information validated concerns about physical space and united the new design with library program needs (Davis and Brown 2012).

## FOCUSING ON MUTUAL CONCERNS

In each of these cases the leadership skills of the librarian created strong partnerships to create mutually beneficial solutions to difficult situations. The teachers at the nationally recognized Blue Ribbon School became an even stronger team; the parent who challenged the book became a library advocate who created a parent group to promote school library needs to the community; and the renovated high school library became a showcase for the district.

### LEADERSHIP TIPS RELATED TO BUILDING STRONG PARTNERSHIPS

▶ Seek solutions that are mutually beneficial.

▶ Know colleagues' strengths.

▶ Understand the school's organizational dynamics.

▶ Anticipate concerns that emanate from fear of loss.

▶ Recognize that negotiation requires developing relationships.

▶ Remember that negotiations are based on the concept that the parties involved must each contribute to the solution.

▶ Seek opportunities to resolve differences.

▶ Be grateful for conflicting or opposing questions and comments.

▶ Bridge ideas to create unity.

▶ Provide research data to support needs.

# Chapter 4

# Consensus through Managing Complexity

Leadership questions related to consensus through managing complexity are:

▶ How does complexity impact decision making?

▶ Are alliances necessary?

▶ Is consensus unanimity?

How did Mike "Coach K" Krzyzewski persuade multimillion-dollar players to set aside their individual basketball aspirations to play for the United States Olympic basketball team in 2008 and again in 2012? Think about this for a minute. To represent the U.S.A. in the Olympic Games, extremely successful professional basketball players agree to play against teams from around the world. Each time these professional basketball players participate in the Olympic Games they put their careers on the line. In 2005 Coach K was chosen to lead the basketball team in the 2008 Olympic Games, and the team successfully earned a gold medal. Since 2005 and prior to the 2012 Olympic Games the team was 52–1 in international play.

Coach K is a leader who understands the importance of developing relationships, reducing complexity among players, using politics to his advantage, and finding platforms to unite players. As coach of the 2012 Olympic basketball team, he was asked if a loss at the Olympic Games in 2012 would smudge his career. His response was, "But not having the opportunity is the worst loss of all" (Whiteside 2012). Risk taking like this is inspirational. By that one comment Coach K persuaded and motivated his team to give up any thoughts of what a loss might do to their careers and, instead, gave them a reason to play.

Whether leading an athletic team to victory or a school staff in effective decision making, leaders who develop relationships know how to reduce complexity and unify members of the group. Organizational complexity results from diverse people with varied opinions, needs, personalities, and goals. The larger the decision-making body the greater the complexity. Lee G. Bolman and Terrence E. Deal have indicated that as complexity in the organization grows there is a need for more sophisticated coordination of strategies (2008). So management must incorporate more-intricate approaches to encourage teamwork as the organization grows. At the same time, too much structure can hinder innovation and creativity. Leaders balance out the complexity of the workforce, the complexity of the organization, and the complexity of the management structure to facilitate agreement.

Decision making depends on mastering how to work through complexity. In school communities soliciting input, communication, and joint decision making from people in the organization is valued. The irony is that the more individual input is encouraged, the greater the complexity that hinders decision making. Successful leaders anticipate organizational complexity, and implement structures and strategies that empower effective and timely decisions.

## REAL-LIFE EXAMPLE

Purchasing databases is one area where librarians need support, not only funding support but also user buy-in. Purchasing something that no one uses is senseless. Insufficient funding is one reality of the school environment. Several years ago, the science department asked me to purchase a science resource to better serve the students' instructional needs. Library funding had not increased. Mulling over the issue, I realized that if one database subscription was canceled to allow purchase of a different resource, one segment of the school would be happy while another would be upset. To avoid alienating any one department, I decided to create a group to assist in the decision.

The first step was to create an online needs-analysis survey, which was sent out to staff and students. Collecting data is one way to reduce complexity because it synthesizes information. The survey results indicated which databases were used most by staff and students. It also showed which databases were valued most by the staff and students. So, while addressing complexity related to differing curriculum needs, the survey did not address the complexity of staff opinions.

At this point I created a committee composed of teachers and students to discuss the situation. The purpose of the first meeting was to explain data from the survey, financial considerations, and different options for purchasing databases for the upcoming year. Making the school library budget public was politically risky because it provided the teachers and students with budget information that was not normally discussed in this school. In addition, this openness confirmed that the library budget was larger than any other department's budget.

So, how could I manage to convince colleagues that the library budget lacked funding to purchase materials due to expanding curriculum needs? It appeared that current resource subscriptions would have to be changed. Allies were needed. Multiple segments of the school had to form a relationship for the good of student instruction. By starting a discussion about students' needs as they relate to instruction, I proceeded to do just that. I knew that increasing student academic achievement was the goal of everyone in the school community, so I collected information connecting the databases to curriculum standards of learning, found where the databases overlapped, and found alternative products containing needed reference information.

The committee reviewed the different databases, and as a group they decided which to purchase. Discussion was focused not on what was going to be lost but on how different sources would serve instructional needs while saving funds. At the same time, I checked with a colleague at a neighboring school and found that if both my school and hers bought certain databases, both schools could receive a discount. This is an example of creating alliances at the building level and reaching out to partner with counterparts in other schools.

All these actions resulted in purchasing databases that met users' needs at a cost that fit the budget. The outcome of having a committee that assisted with decisions about specific databases meant that teachers and students understood the monetary commitment needed to subscribe to the databases. This understanding created value for the resources, and the committee members became supporters for database use. In this case, organizational complexity was minimized by developing relationships, using surveys, and uniting the users by focusing on a common goal. Creating alliances among the different groups within and outside the school worked to solidify the database decision and created broad-based support for the library program.

Committee work-group decision making resulted in all members agreeing to a course of action. Group decision making that seeks consent or consensus means that all can agree to the decision that is made. Consensus is the end goal in some decision making. In political organizations such as schools, consensus is desired because it shows that people within the organization accept an idea. The strength in consensus is that, once achieved, it presents a unified agreement by the group on a particular decision. The weakness of consensus is that it can discourage discussion, innovation, and creativity.

If consensus does not create unanimity until all agree to accept the idea, how do leaders proceed to gain consensus? When a leader strives for consensus, the leader includes all committee members through brainstorming discussion. Brainstorming is the portion of the meeting where members of the group speak freely about issues by providing a quantity of solutions to problems. Brainstorming requires acknowledgment of all ideas without judgment. Eventually, brainstorming leads to combining and reducing solutions until one best result can be agreed upon.

## ANOTHER REAL-LIFE EXAMPLE

A new initiative was being rolled out by my school division relating to the state's waiver from the federal No Child Left Behind law. As district library supervisor, I convened a group of school librarians to discuss tools that would tie individual students' academic achievement to instruction by librarians. During one of the committee meetings a very knowledgeable librarian took over the discussion and did not let any other member of the committee speak. This monopoly completely shut down brainstorming and hindered the work of the committee. When one person talks without letting others contribute to brainstorming, then ideas are lost because participants become involved with listening to one contributor. In this situation, I was able to talk with the librarian and explain the concept of committee and the importance of brainstorming. The librarian had been totally unaware of the detrimental effect of her actions. As supervisor I needed to take leadership of the situation.

In succeeding meetings brainstorming efforts were more balanced. The final decisions on creating tools for librarians to tie individual students' academic achievement to instruction by librarians were made based on synthesis of all committee members' ideas. Group ownership is achieved when all members contribute to the solutions and to the synthesis of ideas. In this situation, unanimity was the result of effective brainstorming that allowed creativity and differing points of view into the discussion. Through brainstorming all members of the committee contributed and consensus was achieved.

## ACHIEVING SUCCESS BY EMBRACING COMPLEXITY

Leaders find ways to merge various elements of complexity in the organization so that unity is achieved. Success is the result of understanding group dynamics and guiding individual people to group decisions that advance a common goal. This goal can be symbolic like the analogy to loss that "Coach K" used or it can be more concrete like achieving student success. Strong alliances enhance decision making by ensuring acceptance of an idea by a group of stakeholders. Leaders who understand organizational complexity know which people are more than likely to band together to form alliances. Effective leaders are able to create alliances based on common interests to make initiatives successful. Although leaders value alliances to move initiatives forward, they also value diverse opinions. Effective leaders allow diverse opinions to surface through the process of brainstorming. Leaders understand that brainstorming unifies complexity of ideas so that consensus in decision making is achieved. Leaders guide members of the organization through unity of purpose by effectively knowing when and how to use symbols, vision, alliances, and brainstorming.

## LEADERSHIP TIPS RELATED TO CONSENSUS BUILDING

▶ Understand that the larger the decision-making body the greater the complexity.

▶ Balance organizational complexity with varied management strategies to facilitate agreement.

▶ Reduce complexity through surveys that synthesize diverse perceptions in a smaller set.

▶ Focus on objectives to inspire unity.

▶ Encourage individual input but expect an increase in complexity.

▶ Create alliances among the different groups within and outside the school to solidify decisions.

▶ Bridging ideas generates broad-based support and forms alliances.

▶ Know that consensus without brainstorming discourages creativity and innovation.

▶ Recognize that the value of consensus is group support for ideas.

▶ Remember that group ownership is achieved when all members contribute to solutions.

# Section 2

# Batman Saves the Day

**DISPOSITIONS**

If you have never had bats in the attic you cannot imagine the sheer fright when a bat flies overhead in such a close environment. Not every pest-control company is willing or able to remove such intruders. It was evident to the owners of the attic that people with special dispositions were needed to resolve this situation. The reality is that bats cannot be exterminated, but they can be relocated. On a warm sunny day, two good-humored guys arrived at the house ready to assess the situation. Their natural curiosity and bat knowledge were evident as they created a plan. One confident batman went up into the attic with the interlopers and a noise maker; the other knowledgeable batman went outside to observe the bats as they left the attic. As soon as the noise began, bats systematically flew out of the attic. Within minutes these calm batmen saved the day and the bats. Sealing the bats' exit after they had left resulted in a permanent fix.

The batmen took leadership of the situation and displayed dispositions that were essential to the performance of their job. Just like these batmen, effective leaders are dependent on acquiring dispositions to manage multiple issues and circumstances related to their job.

# Chapter 5
# Confidence

**Leadership questions related to confidence are:**

▶ What dispositions are related to confidence?

▶ How does self-assessment of dispositions increase leadership success?

▶ How does practicing dispositions deepen beliefs, attitudes, and behaviors?

Marie Kelleher and Michael Phelps are two ends of the age spectrum for competitive swimmers. Both express confidence and courage every day in the pool. Michael Phelps is the most decorated swimmer of all time, who by the age of twenty-seven won six gold and two bronze medals in Athens in 2004, another eight gold medals in Beijing during the 2008 Olympics, and seven more medals in London in 2012. He is known internationally as an accomplished athlete. He works out for hours perfecting his start, strokes, turns, and finishes. He lifts weights; he watches his diet and maintains a strict training regimen. It has been said that when he was in training, he worked out six or more hours a day, six days a week (Wade 2012). Swimming was his job, and he approached it with courage and confidence.

Marie Kelleher is a swimmer too. She swims four days a week and gets up at 5:00 a.m. and drives to the pool for a workout. She swims United States Masters Swimming events, and each year sets swimming records for her age group. Marie Kelleher celebrated her 100th birthday in December 2012. She competes regularly (Holland 2012; Sports Pub. Int'l. 2012).

It takes courage to compete. It takes commitment, managing multiple priorities, and time management to reach excellence in the swimming field. Each day both these athletes display dispositions that make them successful during competition. Practice embeds these dispositions into their actions and thinking. These swimmers are models for how practice deepens beliefs, attitudes, and behaviors.

Think of confidence as an umbrella disposition. Confidence is the umbrella material that forms protection from rain, but the spokes underneath sculpt the strength and contour of the umbrella. If confidence is the umbrella material, then knowledge, commitment, humility, courage, time management, organization, forthrightness, and perseverance are the spokes. Without support material the umbrella will not protect the holder from getting wet, and without spokes the expanse of the umbrella is diminished. Leaders develop confidence in much the same way that Michael Phelps and Marie Kelleher have perfected the disposition. They work hard and practice basic dispositions that build an internal foundation to compete at high levels.

## APPLYING SKILLS LIBRARIANS ALREADY HAVE

### Desire for Knowledge

A continuous desire for knowledge creates a confident leader. This reality is evident because the need for knowledge is constant as job and leadership challenges shift over time. Fortunately, almost all school librarians already have a strong desire for knowledge and the skills needed to acquire it.

When leaders seek new information, their searches are focused in two directions. One focus is aimed at technical skills, and the second is concentrated on dispositions. Leaders understand that knowledge of new job skills is necessary as changes surrounding routine tasks are implemented. Leaders also realize that self-knowledge of their attitudes and beliefs will increase the success or failure of each task. Leaders' self-knowledge results from reflecting on their own proficiencies, limitations, perceptions, and characters. Assessing skills that are done well and those that need improvement is vital for positive job performance. Leaders also reflect on dispositions that affect their work. This reflection is essential because disposition-awareness and how a leader perceives assigned tasks provide a starting point when creating a professional-development plan. Effective professional-development plans are then created to strengthen skills and dispositions. The desire to self-assess dispositions enables leaders to adapt and change as culture and responsibilities grow.

Michael Phelps and Marie Kelleher are not the same swimmers they were ten years ago. Marie does not compete out of town, and she swims shorter events because she does not want to hold anyone up (Howard 2012). At the end of the Beijing Games Michael Phelps took time off because he needed a break from swimming after years of intense training. Two years later he decided to prepare for the London Olympics. He had to reflect on where he was physically and mentally. Michael Phelps knew that to be ready for the 2012 Olympics he had to work out harder than ever because of the compressed timeframe. He decided to focus on weight training. He also listened to his coach Bob Bowman who created a treadmill for swimmers that enabled him to fine-tune Michael's strokes in a short amount of time (Cooper 2012). These are examples of how through self-reflection these swimmers gain knowledge about changes to their needs and how they then match this knowledge with the changing techniques required by their sport. Marie and Michael also examine how their attitudes and beliefs relate to their success in swimming. By practicing new skills and refining dispositions they are able to employ the skills and dispositions to changing circumstances without having to think through each step as if it were in uncharted territory.

Leaders stay up to date through professional development focused on areas in which they know improvement is needed. This focus is the result of employing self-assessing skills and dispositions. Knowledge—including self-knowledge—forms one of the spokes supporting the umbrella disposition of confidence because knowledge is a confidence-builder.

Unwavering leaders are committed to goals, to people, and to success. Their stay-strong professional attitude is bolstered by the belief that common goals unify people toward success. When leaders work with colleagues to establish core beliefs it provides the people in the organization with rationale for goal-setting. School librarians understand the importance of beliefs as a foundation to goal-setting. AASL's *Standards for the 21st-Century Learner* are grounded in nine beliefs (AASL 2007). These beliefs establish a rationale for why school libraries are essential in developing 21st century learners. Librarians' action and commitment to student learning is mapped out through the standards. The AASL *Standards for the 21st-Century Learner* provide school librarians with goals that unified them toward creating a successful instructional program. Leaders that establish goals based on common assumptions and beliefs in the organization create the foundation for successful goal-setting.

## Commitment

A good leader is committed to people in the organization. Fortunately, many librarians were drawn to the profession partly because of their concern for others. Workers feel secure when they know their leader backs them and believes in their contribution to the success of the organization. One outcome of a leader's commitment to people is creation of a safe atmosphere for risk taking. People become motivated to be innovative when fear of making a mistake is not an issue. The spirit and drive behind achieving organizational goals are supported by a committed leader.

Michael Phelps and Marie Kelleher have strengthened their commitment to swimming and their individual success by following through on their training plan, by not giving up, and by believing that their actions will bring success in the pool (Fagan 2012; Holland 2012). Their accomplishments validate this approach. Commitment—believing in goals and acting on those goals—supports confidence when improvement and achievement result.

## Humility

The third spoke of the umbrella is humility. Fortunately, most school librarians are logical thinkers who recognize that leaders who express humility accept success as the result of teamwork rather than taking credit individually for the work of the whole group. Pride in the outcome is a sign that the group is satisfied with their accomplishments. Leaders develop and model humility so colleagues understand that working together brings about successful results. When a leader accepts credit for success without recognizing the people and steps taken to achieve the goal, then the organization will view the leader as arrogant. The leader who has an unassuming nature instills self-respect for his or her leadership and endears the leader to people in the organization. Humility, the third spoke of the umbrella, is strength and inner confidence expressed by a leader who knows his or her role in outcomes.

## Courage

The disposition courage also supports confidence. Leaders need courage to create instructional changes when beliefs focus on quantitative measures that assess a school on how many students pass standardized achievement tests. Inspiring teaching strategies that incorporate critical-thinking and problem-solving skills necessitates a leader with courage to overcome the deeply embedded philosophical practices aimed at memorizing facts.

AASL's *Standards for the 21st-Century Learner* focus on learners who develop skills and self-assessment strategies to become responsible skilled users of information. Courage is needed to motivate change in the school environment and foster this style of instruction. With AASL's *Standards for the 21st-Century Learner* and the resources on the Learning4Life website (AASL 2012), school librarians have the tools and the research results to initiate teaching strategies that foster higher-level thinking. Librarians also have the skills they need to teach students to be critical thinkers. What librarians need is the disposition of courage to make incremental changes to the learning environment. As each change is implemented and success is documented, confidence increases.

As Marie Kelleher continued with her swimming she modified her techniques to suit her current needs. She no longer dives into the pool when starting the race but begins her race at the wall in the pool. The courage to modify a set standard for beginning the race helped her to continue to swim each year. For her the risk is paying off as she continues to be effective in her sport. Likewise, leaders need to develop the disposition of courage that provides them with confidence to meet new challenges.

## Time Management

Time management, the fifth spoke of the umbrella of confidence, is a disposition that is critical to successful leaders. Busy people like school librarians accomplish multiple goals and tasks because they focus on what is important and manage the work until the objectives are completed. Before retiring from competitive swimming, Michael Phelps trained six hours a day, six days a week (Wade 2012). It is hard to imagine how he continued this pace for years leading up to competing in the Olympics in Beijing.

Leaders, like Michael Phelps, develop habits to ensure that the most important tasks are accomplished and decisions are made. A daily or weekly plan is made by reviewing decisions and tasks that require attention. A leader considers the importance of each task and creates an action plan. Leonardo da Vinci said, "Time stays long enough for those who use it" (2012). A leader uses every minute, starting with the most challenging projects and saving the easiest for last. Leaders methodically follow processes and procedures that enable completing projects efficiently. They use calendars, task lists, and e-mail to save time. For example, having a calendar that shows the week at a glance keeps important deadlines handy.

Instead of having to remember multiple milestones, leaders use task lists. These lists keep projects consistently moving toward completion. E-mail saves time when used to seek a quick answer. Turning e-mail off and checking it only periodically throughout the day is another strategy that saves time. Confidence results when objectives are met on time and done well.

## Organization

Leaders not only manage time, they are organized so that time is effectively used. Each day leaders are presented with choices relating to people, tasks, and policies. A leader must be able to organize people and resources so that goals are completed. Being organized is the sixth spoke in the confidence umbrella. Fortunately, all librarians have been taught to organize informational resources. Most can extend these skills to apply to broader organization tasks.

Leaders manage work so it flows from start to finish. They prioritize the incoming requests and long-term goals. They understand where the immediate focus should be and arrange their schedules to ensure that issues are addressed appropriately. Part of being organized is anticipating and gathering the resources needed for a particular job. For example, if a letter must be written, an organized leader anticipates the time it will take to gather the required information and builds time into the plan.

More importantly, effective leaders develop a way to empower others by delegating tasks. This strategy allows leaders to concentrate on tasks that can be accomplished only by them. Leaders let go of control and accept others' contributions to projects. Leaders concentrate on what they do best and delegate to others what those colleagues do best. Both Michael Phelps and Marie Kelleher let their coaches organize practices while they concentrate on doing the swimming. Organizing people and resources, the sixth spoke of the umbrella, creates confidence by enabling deadlines to be met and by accomplishing an efficient work flow.

## Forthrightness

The seventh spoke of the confidence umbrella is forthrightness. A leader who is forthright is admired for candor and frankness. This disposition provides people in the organization with confidence because they know their leader is straightforward and direct, without "hidden agendas." Most librarians are logical thinkers who recognize that forthrightness is particularly important during times of change. Lee G. Bolman and Terrence E. Deal have explained that "change undermines existing structural arrangements, creating ambiguity, confusion and distrust" (2008). A leader who is forthright creates clarity since people in the organization know that what is stated is what needs to happen.

Leaders who are forthright build trust because they address the people, their own actions, and decisions. There is little ambiguity when a leader directly responds to the people in the organization. Vagueness and doubt are eliminated when an organization operates in a consistent manner. When leaders are forthright, respect follows. The seventh spoke of the umbrella, forthrightness, contributes to people having confidence in the leader.

## Perseverance

The eighth spoke of the umbrella is perseverance. Michael Phelps started swimming when he was five years old. The intensity of his workouts grew as he prepared for international competition, and achieved Olympic medals and world records. Although after the Beijing Olympics, Michael took time off to enjoy life, he started training again for the London games two years in advance. He had new obstacles to overcome: gaining endurance and speed in a compressed timeframe (Unger 2012). When leaders tirelessly pursue goals they develop perseverance by building resiliency and determination.

School librarians routinely develop perseverance in students when the librarians probe to find out if students are able to identify another possible source of needed information. The disposition of perseverance strongly supports confidence by rewarding the seeker with answers when, initially, none seemed to be available, or by providing a sense of satisfaction when a goal has been completed when, initially, there seemed to be no way to accomplish it.

Leaders become stronger when they realize that there is always a way to finish a job. Perseverance creates belief in oneself. It assures leaders that they can surmount—or circumvent—obstacles to resolve issues and achieve success. As each objective is accomplished leaders become confident in their ability to work through difficult situations and find solutions. Just as persevering students who are eventually able to answer essential questions gain confidence in their own abilities, leaders who persevere create confidence in their abilities to move the organization forward.

## WIN-WIN SITUATION

Knowledge, commitment, humility, courage, time management, organization, forthrightness, and perseverance build confidence in school librarians who are leaders, but the librarians themselves aren't the only beneficiaries. When school librarians model these dispositions when working with learners, the dispositions are also fostered in students.

Effective school librarians:

- encourage students to self-assess their work to identify areas where more knowledge is needed;
- push students to be committed to an idea and share their information;
- provide opportunities for students to work in teams so they understand humility and the importance of recognizing each contributing member;
- understand that sharing ideas in front of peers requires courage;
- help students learn to manage their time, and prioritize and organize their tasks by insisting that students meet deadlines and goals, and by teaching organizational strategies like the Big 6;

- demand ethical use of information and forthrightness when documenting sources;
- guide learners to persevere and continue to search when answers are not obvious.

These dispositions, when practiced, become habits and build students' confidence. The more the librarian fosters and recognizes these leadership dispositions in students, the more these very same dispositions will become more obvious to the librarian. Just as a confident learner is the outcome of these practiced dispositions, a confident leader develops as well.

## LEADERSHIP TIPS RELATED TO CONFIDENCE

- ▶ Practice dispositions to embed them in actions and thinking.
- ▶ Remember that seeking and acquiring knowledge create a confident leader.
- ▶ Self-assess skills and dispositions to identify areas to strengthen.
- ▶ Recognize that unwavering attitudes inspire action.
- ▶ Gain respect by accepting success as the result of teamwork rather than taking credit individually for the work of the whole group.
- ▶ Develop courage by stepping out to make incremental changes to achieve larger objectives.
- ▶ Anticipate and gather resources for a particular job; this preparation results in effective time management.
- ▶ Eliminate vagueness and doubt by being direct and forthright.
- ▶ Develop perseverance to build resiliency and determination.
- ▶ Remember that leading an organization requires practicing dispositions that create confidence.

# Chapter 6
## Coaching

**Leadership questions related to coaching are:**

▶ Is coaching a leadership model?

▶ How important are dispositions to coaches?

▶ What role does coaching have in leadership?

What do John Wooden, Pat Summitt, and Vince Lombardi have in common besides being coaches of highly successful teams? Each of these coaches wrote a book that provides insight into leadership. Documenting their coaching philosophy and strategies in leadership books is not surprising because successful coaches use leadership skills to form individuals into teams. Coaches know the big picture, develop trust and respect, make reasonable demands, hold others accountable, delegate work, and develop individuals. They are often self-directed and are active listeners who value others' opinions and differing perspectives. Successful coaches understand that leadership is not demanding action, but, instead, is instilling discipline, self-respect, and attitudes in each player. John Wooden, Pat Summitt, and Vince

Lombardi taught their players leadership principles that could be applied to leadership in all aspects of life.

Coaches scan the team, the competition, and the schedule to get a big picture of what the season ahead will require. Knowing the big picture is important to leaders because it defines the dispositions employees need for the organization to achieve defined outcomes. Leaders must provide a vision and then inspire the actions necessary for success. This provision of vision and inspiration is what John Wooden did when he developed his teams.

John Wooden created what he termed the "Pyramid of Success" (CBS 2010). In this model he described what it takes to achieve competitive greatness. What is interesting about his pyramid is that each level of the pyramid is packed with dispositional qualities. John Wooden knew that skills are essential, but an individual's disposition can destroy or build a team. He cited "industriousness, friendship, loyalty, cooperation and enthusiasm" as the foundations of success (CBS 2010). He knew that championship teams do not result unless all players express these attitudes. As he continued up the pyramid he then listed "self-control, alertness, initiative and intentness; condition, skill and team spirit; and poise and confidence" as the next tier leading to success (CBS 2010). Wooden identified the pinnacle as competitive greatness, which he defined as "performing at one's best ability when one's best is required, which, he said, was each day" (CBS 2010). His exemplary achievements are difficult for any player or coach to match.

He knew that success was dependent upon dispositions. It makes sense that leaders can learn something from the coach. Leaders are coaches of a team of workers. They must display dispositions that they wish their colleagues to display. By instilling these same attitudes in colleagues, leaders create a foundation for an accomplished organization.

## TRUST AND RESPECT

Trust and respect are reciprocal in high-achieving organizations. Trust and respect are dispositions that are developed over time as a result of consistent, honest decisions and actions. Leaders who are truthful gain respect. Pat Summitt, coach of the University of Tennessee women's basketball team and one of the most winning coaches of all time, used what she termed the "Definite Dozen" with her teams. The very first item on her list is "respect yourself and others" (Summitt 1999, 8). By the time she wrote *Reach for the Summit* she was well respected for her ability to coach women's basketball. In this book she explains how she learned that respect cannot be demanded or beaten out of people; instead, it needs to be cultivated. She goes on to state that team cohesion is built on respect (Summitt 1999, 12). When Pat Summitt talked about respect she meant respect for rules, others, and oneself.

Good leaders establish rules to create efficiency and stability. Just as coaches create game plans, leaders also create plans that need to be followed. To follow the plan, players must respect the coach. A loss results when teams fall apart because each player thinks he or she knows more than the leader. The game plan also disintegrates when players do not respect teammates.

When I was a high school librarian, one year the girls' basketball team had two superstars. These two players knew they could score points. In one particular game they proceeded to run and gun the ball. In spite of the coach's benching them for a time, they did not listen to the game plan. Their disrespect seemed to work for a while until the opposing team started double-teaming the two stars. All of a sudden it did not matter that these two were great shooters; no baskets were being made. These stars needed to trust the other players. Trust means knowing the person will perform and get the job done according to plan. Respect for talents of colleagues results in team accomplishments.

Another difficult situation for leaders and coaches is when individuals do not fully respect their own expertise. Without self-respect the team falters because all members of the team must believe in themselves to execute skills to accomplish objectives. Belief in oneself builds self-confidence and, consequently, team confidence. A winning team succeeds or fails based on the level of trust and respect team members give themselves and each other.

## TWO-WAY STREET

Coaches who make reasonable demands while pushing players to higher levels of performance are valued. Coach Vince Lombardi placed great emphasis on practice. In the book *The Lombardi Rules* he related how he would run the same play over and over again until the players got it right. He knew that each team member needed to perform fundamentals on the field often so their actions were automatic responses to plays (Lombardi 2002, 256–64).

He stressed that the discipline of hard work and training leads to mastery of skills. Coach Lombardi made demands during practice so his players stayed focused and made tough decisions during games.

Leaders often ask colleagues to perform tasks that require going beyond their job descriptions. Tasks that encourage opportunities for colleagues to master and grow more proficient in their jobs are realistic—especially when team members know the coach is expending extra effort. Coach Vince Lombardi's players knew he would spend hours working late into the night on game plans, and reviewing game tapes (Lombardi 2002, 250–56), Although the players were being pushed, they knew their coach was pushing himself hard as well. It is reasonable to ask colleagues to perform work that drills for mastery when the leader models the same commitment in the work.

## ACCOUNTABILITY

Related to increased responsibility is holding colleagues accountable for the work they perform. At game time coaches have rosters, game plans, and scouting reports. Once play starts the players are accountable for implementing the game plan and understanding their roles on the team. Players on the bench understand their role as well, for without the breadth and depth of teammates, practice and substitutions are not possible. If each person on a team is accountable for an assigned role, then opportunity for success is high.

Like sports' coaches, leaders also use rosters, provide a game plan, and research data related to initiatives. They hold every member of the organization accountable to accomplish his or her specific role. Accountability is performing the job and finishing each task with high proficiency. When leaders measure colleagues' actions against a standard, those colleagues are provided with information about deficiencies as well as successes. A coach and a leader measures actions, results, and efficiency. The information gathered when these measures are applied helps leaders create plans to achieve future goals.

## DELEGATION

Coaches have assistants, trainers, and managers who support the vision of the team. Delegating work to staff creates an opportunity for those with specific skills to make the team better. In sports, assistants concentrate on one aspect of the sport, and coaches trust assistants to complete their jobs. Leaders in organizations likewise have assistants. Leaders break up larger tasks into smaller jobs and assign these smaller jobs to colleagues with expertise in these areas. Success comes when a leader or coach respects teammates enough to effectively delegate work. The leader or coach shares the acclaim for successes, but accepts ultimate responsibility for sub-par results.

## DEVELOPING FUTURE LEADERS

Succession plans are critical to organizations. When individuals' talents are developed and diversified, then the organization is stronger. Often an assistant coach replaces a head coach. This succession is a sign that the assistant knows the team and what is important to the owners of the team. It makes sense to ensure that there is overlap in responsibilities so the organization can continue to operate should a leader leave.

Developing individuals into leaders requires coaching. This development necessitates providing training and increased responsibility. It also involves identifying people for those roles, as well as providing opportunities for specific experiences that are needed for each job. Leaders who prepare leaders from within demonstrate respect for their colleagues' abilities and plan for the future.

## WIN-WIN SITUATION

John Wooden, Pat Summitt, and Vince Lombardi are examples of exemplary coaches as evidenced by their records and honors. They were not only great coaches, they were great leaders. They led team after team to victory by embedding leadership dispositions into goals. Vince Lombardi's son explained that his father "motivated and inspired his players to surpass their own perceived physical and mental capability" (Lombardi 2002, paragraph 75–85). Any leaders can learn from these coaches. Vince Lombardi stated that "Leadership rests not only on outstanding ability, but on commitment, loyalty, pride, and followers ready to accept guidance" (Lombardi 2008, 91–92).

Coaching is dependent on dispositional training. The books describing the philosophy and dispositions admired and cultivated by John Wooden, Pat Summitt, and Vince Lombardi clearly illustrate how important it is for members of teams to have attitudes that support the skills needed to perform the job. Coach after coach stresses the importance of knowing the big picture, developing trust and respect, making reasonable demands, holding others accountable, delegating work, and developing individuals. Of course, helping team members develop dispositions that lead to success paid off for the coaches. However, the coaches' efforts paid off for the players, too. Not only did the players have the satisfaction (and, sometimes, financial rewards) associated with winning, the players also developed dispositions that are transferrable to other areas of their lives. Your leadership can have similar benefits to members of your team.

## LEADERSHIP TIPS RELATED TO COACHING

▶ Remember that valuing others' opinions and differing perspectives is important to coaches.

▶ Instill the same attitudes in colleagues that coaches consider important for success; you will create an accomplished organization.

▶ Respect the talents of colleagues, and team accomplishments will result.

▶ Recognize that belief in oneself builds self-confidence and team confidence.

▶ Encourage hard work and training, which lead to mastery of skills.

▶ Hold team members accountability not just for performing the job but for finishing each task with high proficiency.

▶ Delegate work and share glory for success, but accept that as leader you have ultimate responsibility for successes and failures.

▶ Develop individuals into leaders by coaching them.

▶ Learn from the dedication and hard work that coaches require.

▶ Recognize that it is reasonable to ask colleagues to perform work that drills for mastery when the leader models the same commitment in the work.

# Chapter 7

# Humor

**Leadership questions related to using humor are:**

▶ When is humor appropriate at work?

▶ What guidelines are important when using humor?

▶ How does humor impact leadership?

It was the end of the school year, and a high school librarian was retiring. The student newspaper always ran an article about staff retirees in their final edition for the year. So a student reporter asked the librarian, "Why did you become a librarian?" The librarian responded that back when she was deciding what to do with her life she had limited choices. She could have become a secretary, but she didn't want to type all day. She could have become a nurse, but she did not want to see half-naked people all day, or she could have become a teacher, but she did not want to tell kids what to do all day. So, she became a librarian. She went on to tell the student reporter that now, many years later, "I spend all day typing on a computer, telling half-naked kids what to do" (Ragland 2012).

When the librarian explained why she chose librarianship she took the reality of her limited life choices and turned it into something humorous. This story was shared at a library district-level end-of-the-year meeting and set the mood for fun. The complete truth of the comments, presented stoically, resulted in hearty laughter.

## USING HUMOR WISELY

Humor is used at work as a communication tool to lighten burdensome situations, to explain difficult concepts, to soften bad news, to refocus attention, to motivate, and to encourage a more-human understanding of a leader. Used appropriately, humor explains the organization, clarifies initiatives, and inspires teamwork. Leaders who direct humor at themselves exhibit strength and humility that allow colleagues to better understand them. Humor is a stress reliever and changes the pace of meetings by redirecting colleagues when issues are off topic. A leader must understand how to use humor effectively.

Humor should never be used to threaten. When a leader makes a cutting comment, receives a silent or passive reaction, and then says, "It's a joke, it's a joke," it is not. When an audience has to be told a joke is a joke, it isn't. Humor is intended to lift moods, people, and the organization. When humor is divisive, disparaging, hostile, or attacking, it ceases to be effective. A guideline when using humor is to lighten the mood while providing well-intentioned messages.

Another guideline for leaders to follow when using humor is to refrain from using offensive language. A good leader reads his audience and watches expressions on colleagues' faces. Using off-color remarks is not an appropriate choice when inserting humor into a business environment. Leaders understand that humor is a powerful communication strategy when a situation, story, or remark is described without using foul or intimidating language. The key to effective use of humor in the workplace is understanding when and how to insert it appropriately into the daily activities of the organization.

## LIGHTEN BURDENS

Billy Graham noted that "a keen sense of humor helps us to overlook the unbecoming, understand the unconventional, tolerate the unpleasant, overcome the unexpected, and outlast the unbearable" (Graham 2012). School librarians are sometime faced with unbecoming, unconventional, unpleasant, unexpected and unbearable situations. A sense of humor redirects these events and places them in perspective. An example is the time two librarians in a middle school were cleaning their equipment room—a task that is always unpleasant. One librarian asked the second librarian about a mike stand that was in two pieces. After looking at the two pieces she said, "Is this broken?" The second librarian responded, "No, it just doesn't work" (Howe and Marquis 2012). Cleaning out the room eliminates unused, dated, and broken equipment. It required heavy lifting in a dusty environment, culminating in making final decisions. In this situation humor lightened the mood and made the task bearable.

## MAKE POINTS EFFECTIVELY

Another purpose of humor is to transform absurdities into more realistic situations. Leaders know that even good initiatives tend to have a ridiculous side to them. I worked in a district where some middle schools were staffed with a 1.5 library position. This meant that several days a week the library was staffed with a full-time librarian and an additional librarian. On the remaining days of the week the .5 librarian was at another middle school. This situation created confusion and imbalance to the services offered, and, despite several very creative solutions, the schools came up short on consistent service to students and staff.

As district supervisor I documented turnover and success of this accommodation at each of the impacted schools. I decided to ask for two full-time positions for each of the middle schools and went to the assistant superintendent for instruction. I provided detailed data showing need for additional staffing, but it was difficult to create a picture of how having two full-time librarians some days created expectations that couldn't be met on the days when only one librarian was available. Finally, I provided this description. I explained that I asked the librarians to put a sign at the entrance to the library on the days when the additional librarian was not there. The sign read, "Today there are only half the librarians available so half of the students in your group need to return to class." It was a fairly ridiculous statement, but it made the assistant superintendent laugh. In the end, the assistant superintendent understood the analogy better than all the data that was previously provided. This humor explained the distinct difference between what was intended and what actually ended up happening in libraries with unequal staffing.

## SOFTEN BAD NEWS

Leaders may use humor to soften bad news. Budget news for school districts is increasingly difficult to deliver since the world-wide economic problems began around 2007. It is challenging to repeatedly guide colleagues to feel good about decreasing resources. The changes resulting from each budget year's allocation begin to get old. So, as a library supervisor, I was explaining that as a result of changing database providers the information resources would look different; teaching how to use these new resources would need to be revised, too. However, the good news was that, although we were going to a different provider, the quality of the resources was comparable. The librarians understood the need to change, yet, as supervisor, I could feel their disappointment over losing familiar resources. At this point, I said, "A friend of mine told me that her best years came from the times when she had little money. So, in my estimation we should be headed toward really great times as we move through this economy." The laughter broke the tension in the room. Humor helped move the meeting forward.

## REFOCUS ATTENTION

To introduce a lighter spirit when needed, leaders incorporate humor strategically when communicating with colleagues. Sometimes heavy discussions sidetrack meetings, especially if attendees have experienced problems related to the topic at hand. Although the leader's intention is only to communicate information and then move on to other topics, attendees may seize the opportunity to vent. Humor can get the meeting back on track.

An example was when, as a library supervisor, I was explaining the forms and procedures for getting rid of surplus materials and equipment. The librarians started expressing concern about the volume of old materials that were being stored in the school library for months, waiting to go to the warehouse. It was beginning to look like each of the eighty-two librarians was going to comment about their personal trauma dealing with surplus material, but one attendee helped get the meeting back on track. She stood up and said, "I have a problem that everyone here needs to know about. It began several years ago when I started getting too many paper clips. I have paper clips in every drawer in the library. I want to know how to 'surplus' all these paper clips!" (Ragland 2012).

In a very subtle way this librarian made the point that everyone has problems with surplus items. The librarians understood the humor and began asking her to send paper clips to them. This perceptive use of humor allowed the librarians to see how silly their concerns were in relation to the more important issues that had to be addressed.

## MOTIVATE

Humor serves as a motivator. Leaders who are aware of the level of stress in the organization use humor to motivate, enhance teamwork, and inspire creativity. Although humor is often verbal, it is also expressed through events that motivate. Librarians often use humor in school-wide events. An elementary librarian was charged with encouraging an increased love of reading. She created an event called the Great Pig Race. Every class reads books all year. Toward the end of the year the students talk about books they have read and discuss their favorite characters. The librarian provides each grade level with a battery-operated toy pig to dress. The students on each grade level vote on a character and dress the pig as that character (Hally 2012). On a specified day, the pigs race each other to see which pig wins the Great Pig Race.

Teachers, administrators, and students bought into reading, dressing a pig, and wanting their pig to win the Great Pig Race. Though this event is meant to encourage reading, it has additional benefits. The entire school comes together to make the pig race a success. After three years the Great Pig Race is so important that now the race is video-streamed so parents can tune in and watch the event live (Fitzpatrick and Tuckwiller 2012). The release of energy, the creativity of the decorated pigs, and the whole school working together encourage reading, and the event is a team builder for the school. Leaders create events and opportunities from silly-hat day to team-spirit days that incorporate fun and humor to motivate colleagues.

## ENHANCE LEADERSHIP

It takes a confident leader to see humor in his or her actions. Often leaders like this are in a good mood and fun to be around. Colleagues welcome a leader who laughs at his or her own mistakes. The ability to laugh at oneself exposes a part of a leader's personality that makes the leader seem more human. In August 2011, *Time* magazine reported on the results of a study by Ursula Beermann of the University of California, Berkeley, and Willibald Ruch of the University of Zurich. They studied seventy psychology students to gauge their ability to laugh at themselves. "The findings support what has long been believed: that being able to laugh at oneself is not only a distinct trait, but is also linked with having an upbeat personality and good mood and may be the foundation for a good sense of humor" (Szalavitz 2011).

Colleagues, in turn, value an environment that enables them freedom to laugh at themselves because it creates an overall feeling of wellbeing. Based on Beermann and Ruch's study, leaders who have the ability to laugh at their own actions often possess the easygoing personality needed when developing a humorous disposition.

Humor as a disposition positively impacts leadership. A 2011 study in Taiwan showed that humorous leadership in the workplace resulted in "lowered stress at work; helped subordinates understand leaders' management models through the communication between them, and inspired subordinates or followers" (Ho et al. 2011). The increasing intensity and pace in the workplace today indicates the disposition of humor is needed by leaders. Humor creates an atmosphere where tension is lessened and people become motivated. The Great Pig Race shows how humor creates an environment where creativity and innovation are the outcomes. When a leader finds humor in events and conveys this to colleagues, then news—good and bad—is more palatable. Humor is most effective when it is expressed in an ethical and professional manner. In the end, humor helps leaders establish and maintain an amiable relationship with their subordinates and further boost their leadership (Ho et al. 2011).

## LEADERSHIP TIPS RELATED TO USING HUMOR

▶ Remember that humor helps to explain the organization, clarifies initiatives, inspires teamwork, and motivates colleagues.

▶ Convey humor in an ethical and professional manner for greatest effectiveness.

▶ Recognize that using humor in a divisive, disparaging, hostile, or attacking manner is ineffective.

▶ Be aware of the level of stress in the organization and use humor to motivate, enhance teamwork, and inspire creativity.

▶ Use humor to redirect the flow of meetings that have gotten off topic.

▶ Wield humor appropriately as a powerful communication strategy.

▶ Direct humor at yourself to exhibit strength and humility that allow colleagues to better understand you.

▶ Use humor to transform absurdities into more realistic situations.

▶ Incorporate humor strategically to introduce a lighter spirit.

▶ Remember that the key to effective use of humor in the workplace is understanding when and how to insert it appropriately into the daily activities of the organization.

# Chapter 8

# Authenticity

**Leadership questions related to authenticity are:**

▶ Which dispositions are needed to be authentic?

▶ How does authenticity enhance leadership?

▶ What does authenticity have to do with the concept of branding?

An effective leader exhibits many dispositions. Being authentic is the most powerful leadership disposition. Authenticity is complicated because it is not just one disposition but many. To be authentic, leaders must model honesty, integrity, dependability, ethics, and sound judgment.

Authenticity is essential when searching for collectibles and name-brand products. Without certain identifying marks and unique qualities an article may not be authentic. Television shows abound where either the stars of the show are looking for unique pieces that are in demand for resale or people are bringing items found in their attics to pawnbrokers to assess each object's value.

Creating markers that identify products such as Apple devices, Nike apparel and shoes, and Gorham silver is done to assure purchasers a certain level of quality. With so many products competing for customers, items with identifying marks and certificates validating their authenticity have an advantage in the marketplace.

Authenticity goes beyond the name on the product and the logo. Customers value a product for unique design and service. Authenticity is dependent on multiple factors that brand a product. In the same vein, branding leaders as authentic means they show evidence of intrinsically embedded dispositions that imbue their actions and decisions with value.

Branding is more than a name, more than a logo. Branding is the company's vision explained to consumers, often through a pithy slogan. "More importantly it is the value customers ascribe to a product. Brand always answers the question 'who am I?' It is the way the company differentiates itself from its competition" (Dougherty 2010). Colleagues ascribe a value to leaders. A leader's most powerful branding is authenticity. A leader's style has markers and indicators that brand him or her as authentic. Leaders exhibit dispositions such as honesty, integrity, dependability, ethics, and sound judgment. These dispositions are the bedrock of authenticity and give legitimacy to leadership skills by instilling trust in leaders' actions and decisions.

Apple branding is tied to its logo and to the idea of innovation. One reason consumers purchase Apple products such as the iPad, iPhone, and MacBook Pro is because Apple Inc. is known for being innovative. In 2008 Apple entered nine products into the International Forum Product Design awards competition. Out of the nine products, eight won awards, and seven of the eight were gold awards (Berka 2008). Companies prove their authenticity with awards, certificates, and records. The bottom line for product success is how well consumers believe the company's branding. A leader's success is dependent on how well colleagues believe in the leader.

Just as Apple Inc. developed multiple products that, over time, won consumers' loyalty, leaders develop loyal colleagues through leadership that demonstrates the authenticity dispositions. In organizations every action by their leaders leaves an imprint defining the extent of their authenticity.

## BENEFITS

A leader who is genuine is committed to using—and fostering in others—the key dispositions that support authenticity. For example, military leaders stress and embed a strict code of ethics into basic training. Logos of armed forces are well recognized, and their slogans are too. *Semper Fidelis*, the motto of the U.S. Marine Corps, means "Always Faithful" (U.S. Marine Corps 2012). In 2006 the U.S. Army unveiled a new slogan, "Army Strong." Both forces hope to attract recruits who believe what the branding conveys (Norris 2006). Both branches of the armed forces want to be known for a commitment to dispositions that create fidelity and strength.

Their code includes honesty, integrity, loyalty, accountability, fairness, caring, respect, promise keeping, responsible citizenship, and pursuit of excellence (U.S. Dept. of Defense 2011, 119). All recruits learn the importance of these values because others' lives depend on their actions and decisions. As a result, recruits are expected to live these dispositions daily so that in battle and other real-life crisis situations they exhibit the internalized dispositions that allow marines and soldiers to embody these values.

In civilian life, too, successful leaders are committed to making decisions that are based on the deep-rooted values that create authentic leadership. When dispositions such as honesty, integrity, dependability, ethics, and sound judgment are consistently displayed by leaders, these values are evident in all levels of management and within the members of the organization.

## HONESTY

Among the primary dispositions stressed by the U.S. Army are "being truthful, straightforward and candid," which are characteristics of honesty (U.S. Dept. of Defense 2011, 118). Honesty invokes trust and respect in both military and civilian settings. In 1994 a movie came out entitled *True Lies*. The play on words gives viewers insight into the movie's plot, which waivers between suspense and comedy as the main character, a "mild mannered computer salesman" transforms into a "multilingual super-operative for Omega Sector, a secret government agency in Washington" (Howe 1994). His wife is none the wiser until an incident brings his lie to the truth as she becomes involved in helping solve an international situation. The title of the movie raises questions about how—and whether—a lie can be true.

Leaders, of course, know that a lie can't be true; any distortion of truth creates deceptiveness. Dishonesty and lies resonate poorly with people in organizations because "lies erode credibility and undermine public confidence"

(U.S. Dept. of Defense 2011, 118). Therefore, honesty resonates well with people in organizations because truth provides confidence and clarity. Clarity enables colleagues to focus on accomplishing goals to be fulfilled rather than having to sort through underhanded, manipulative directives. True lies may make an interesting title for a movie, but they have no place in leadership.

## INTEGRITY

A good leader knows that integrity creates organizational certainty and collegial confidence. Integrity deepens authenticity because integrity is the manifestation of internal beliefs revealed through actions a leader performs and words a leader speaks. Personal actions and decisions follow principles deeply entrenched in the character of the leader. Just as members of the armed forces expect military leaders to express the military code of ethics when making life and death decisions, colleagues depend on consistency and reliability in their leaders' actions, reactions, and directives.

They also expect a leader to be impartial and open-minded. Fair and balanced decisions when issuing statements and meeting responsibilities are characteristics of integrity. Leaders with integrity are unbiased when directing the organization and its people. They pass decisions through an internal filter, critiquing their own rationales to ensure honesty. A leader who meets his or her individual expectations for integrity is able to display that disposition to others—and inspire it in others, too.

## DEPENDABILITY

Dependability is a disposition that creates stability, calmness, and confidence. A Google search for "dependable car repair" brings up company after company that has the word "dependable" in its name. When a car breaks down on the side of the road, finding a dependable auto repair shop is the driver's primary concern. Choosing a car mechanic often relies on validation that the mechanic is knowledgeable, reliable, and provides consistently high-quality work. An auto-repair company is valued when it has a great reputation for providing trustworthy advice when a car breaks down. A good car mechanic provides data and evidence that the brakes on the car need repair not replacement, that the air conditioner needs a part not an entirely new unit, or that the noise is the result of normal wear and tear and requires no work. A dependable car mechanic consistently provides accurate identification of the problem. In addition, the car runs smoothly and does not break down after being fixed. And, when a driver is looking for a new car, the mechanic can be trusted to provide advice on which make and model of a car is the best buy based on the repair history of different makes and models.

Leaders, too, must be dependable. Like a car mechanic, leaders must be reliable, consistent, and knowledgeable. It is essential that colleagues know when a task needs refinement not replacement, an initiative requires an extra step not a complete revision, or that responsibilities are a part of daily duties. Just as a mechanic gains customers as a result of his reputation, a dependable leader attracts good people to his or her organization because the leader is trustworthy.

## ETHICS

Ethics are an all or nothing disposition. Speed limits are intended to protect and apply to all drivers. In April of 2011, the Idaho State Police started a campaign to stop speeding. They branded their campaign with the slogan "Stop Speeding Before it Stops You" (Idaho State Police 2011). This slogan conveys a clear picture of the danger of speeding. Assuming that the speedometer on the car is accurate, the driver knows whether he or she is driving the car too fast. There are no shades of gray; the driver is speeding or not.

Ethics work the same way. A person cannot be a little unethical. A person is either ethical or not. Ethical limits are set by organizations. These limits are typically outlined in policies and procedures manuals. Leaders know where these guidelines are and refer to them. These guidelines ensure leaders' actions and decisions are within the acceptable limits of the organization. Actions intentionally taken outside these limits, these guiding principles of the organization, are unethical.

Deciding to be ethical is a commitment to moral authenticity. At some time or another, problems arise that could be resolved more quickly and easily by bending or breaking a rule set out in an organizational policy or procedure. Although by breaking a rule the situation may be resolved quickly, this resolution has the potential to be a short-term solution that eventually ends up creating larger, more complex problems to solve. Eliminating unethical solutions and taking time to achieve results while adhering to principles provide permanence and authenticity to a leader's credibility.

## SOUND JUDGMENT

Sound judgment on the surface seems easy and logical to employ. It is the result of gathering information, assessing data, measuring ideas against policy, and deciding objectively. Using specific steps to create and then implement a strategy is a routine action. Whether leaders are making simple or complex decisions the process is the same. Leaders follow a pattern that results in good decisions. This process works well for everyday decision making, but at some point an emergency will arise when a leader needs to almost instantly decide on a course of action. During a crisis, emotions become a factor in the decision-making process. It is during these times that sound judgment based on set procedures is needed but difficult to employ dispassionately.

Hurricane Katrina's landing in New Orleans on August 29, 2005, brought heavy rain of over one inch an hour while wind speeds were recorded at over 140 mph. The loss of life and damage to New Orleans was intensified when the levee broke leaving some parts of New Orleans under twenty feet of water (NOAA 2005). This one event exemplifies many opportunities the inhabitants and the leadership of the Louisiana community had to use sound judgment. The difficulty with sound judgment is that often emotion and past experiences color the decision-making process. When having to make a quick decision the same process of gathering data, analyzing options, and following a plan of action needs to be spontaneously and rapidly followed.

During Hurricane Katrina sound judgment was clouded by past experience and an inability to comprehend and address a catastrophic event. Leaders mentally train how to make sound judgments through using set processes during simpler, less intense decisions so that when a more complex resolution is needed, their skills enable them to think ahead and consider the impact their actions have on others. Genuine leaders have the ability to see a wider view of the problem than what appears on the surface and to take time to lead others to the right outcome. Processes lead to sound conclusions by taking the emotion out of situations. Leaders understand that decisions become an automatic response based on verified data when decision-making steps are practiced.

## BENEFITS

Coca-Cola is one of the most recognized brands in the world. This company is committed to promoting a brand that is identified by its logo, unique bottle design, and advertising campaigns. One of its most effective campaigns "It's the Real Thing" was intended to let consumers know that their product was the authentic cola among all the competing brands.

Leaders need to convey the message that they are the real thing, authentic in actions and words. To create an authentic leadership style, leaders cultivate dispositions such as honesty, integrity, dependability, ethics, and sound judgment. They do this through self-reflection, following standards in place, and practicing vetted processes. Leaders use each of these dispositions as a routine part of their daily activities.

What's the payoff? Companies and leaders thrive on authenticity. Goals are met. Expectations are exceeded. Organizations' success is dependent on creating a brand that consumers relate to and see as a symbol of excellence. Leaders' success is equally dependent on creating a brand that colleagues trust and believe. A leader who is authentic receives respect, workforce stability, and consistent results. If a brand answers the question, "Who am I?" then colleagues should be able to define their leader's dispositions as honesty, integrity, dependability, and ethics. The ultimate beneficiaries of authentic leadership are the people served—in our case, learners and other educators.

## LEADERSHIP TIPS RELATED TO AUTHENTICITY

▶ Display authenticity to fulfill colleagues' need for sincerity and clarity.

▶ Remember that leaders' actions leave an imprint that explains how they manage.

▶ Develop loyal colleagues through leadership actions that are honest and ethical.

▶ Recognize that a leader's success is dependent on how well colleagues believe in the leader.

▶ Issue statements and responsibilities that are fair and balanced; these are indicators of integrity.

▶ Be honest; people can recognize when a leader is not honest.

▶ Cultivate the dispositions of authentic leaders; be dependable, reliable, consistent, and knowledgeable.

▶ Outline ethical limits in organizational policies and procedures.

▶ Establish and use processes for daily decisions to make sound judgments.

▶ Have predetermined procedures that take the emotion out of situations.

# Section 3

# Reserved for Parties of Three or More

**COMMUNICATION**

Words are powerful and their use conveys meaning that drives actions and reactions. After taking my granddaughters to a play I decided to top the afternoon off by going to Café Guttenberg, a quaint restaurant with tables surrounded by shelves of books. This restaurant is a seat-yourself environment, so we went to a table in the back room. On the middle of the table in a framed placard were the words, "This table is reserved for parties of three or more." My granddaughter Sydney said, "Grandma, we can't sit here." When I asked why, she pointed to the framed message. And I explained that since there were four of us it was okay for us to sit there. Then she pointed to the words "reserved for parties" and said, "We are not having a party." I then explained that in this case the party meant a group not a social event. She was still rather young to understand that this word had two meanings so I finally said that we would make our visit a party!

Articulating information in understandable ways removes tangled layers conveyed by words. Leadership is dependent on clear, focused, and result-driven communication of messages that minimizes misconceptions of human thinking.

# Chapter 9

# Preparedness

**Leadership questions related to preparedness in the context of communication are:**

▶ How do digital communication tools impact preparedness?

▶ What do leaders consider when preparing to communicate information?

▶ How do leaders determine the best format for the message?

Preparedness is being in a state of readiness. A family getting ready for a beach vacation investigates possible locations, makes a checklist of what to bring, gathers and packs the items, and decides on the best route to travel before starting out. Parents are thoughtful as they cover each point in the preparation phase for the vacation. The end goal is to arrive at the beach with food, clothes, chairs, floats, toys, suntan lotion, and, perhaps a hundred other items that will make the stay at the beach successful. It may seem obvious that a vacation needs preparation. After all, nothing is worse than arriving at the beach without an essential like suntan lotion or sunglasses. When an event like a beach trip or an action like communication is important to a group of people, then preparation facilitates success.

Knowing about changes to beach equipment is important to the preparations for a beach trip. Knowing about changes in communication is important to leaders when communicating. In the twenty-first century, communication is often immediate. The impact of the computer and digital communication changes how and when leaders communicate news, events, and directives. Without practice and preparation, a leader is at a disadvantage when using digital tools. Colin Powell wanted to change his own skill set by adding laptop computers to the State Department offices. He tried to persuade the entire State Department that communication had changed and was no longer bound by time. He also understood that work demanded immediate action because efforts were no longer "measured by clocks and the passage of days" (Powell 2012, 109). Communication time is no longer measured by the speed of mail trucks and the passage of days and weeks. Yesterday's tools such as landline phones and postal letters have morphed into smart mobile phones, e-mail, and text messages. Television and the Internet instantly convey news from around the world, communicating events uninterruptedly around the clock. Breaking news comes to smartphones via alerts and messages. The instantaneous nature of communication means leaders must always be in a state of readiness to respond to colleagues' need for information.

Social networking provides instant information in an environment in which Facebook and Twitter communicate real-time information about events happening around the world. For example, in 2011 an earthquake rocked the little town of Louisa, Virginia. Communities along the East Coast as far away as Maine felt the tremors. Louisa is about fifteen miles from where I was when the earthquake hit. Phone lines were jammed; news media wanted to confirm what was taking place, but I first found out from my Facebook friends what was really happening. Instantly, I was able to react and seek safety.

A leader's job is to be prepared with correct information, to know how to use up-to-date tools appropriately, and to communicate information in a timely manner. Some of the vacation items I took to the beach twenty years ago are still among the items packed in the car for 21st-century beach trips, but as technology has changed additional and different items are brought along. The simple beach umbrella now has an additional gadget that anchors the umbrella deep in the sand to withstand wind gusts. Knowing that this tool is available is my job as a parent and responsible beach-goer. I no longer worry that the umbrella will go flying across the beach and possibly hurt someone. When communicating, a leader's job is to keep up with advances in the means of dissemination of information. This necessity raises the art of communication to a whole new level because unexpected problems, like those caused by a flying umbrella, occur when communication is late or delivered inappropriately.

## HUMAN GPS

A leader must be the Global Positioning System (GPS) of the organization's communication network, and be prepared to sort information and communicate what is pertinent. A navigation system is increasingly important as a tool for helping people arrive at their destinations. GPS devices also provide peripheral information about where to find a gas station, a restaurant, or shopping venues. Similarly, to direct colleagues a leader needs to be prepared to communicate basic information, as well as additional useful information, so that work is completed smoothly and efficiently.

Once a GPS has been activated, the user is fairly confident that correct and efficient directions will be provided. Several road choices may be offered to get the user to the desired destination. One choice may be a faster route over newer interstate highways, and another choice may be a shorter distance with more traditional in-town driving. The user picks the route based on his or her personal situation. For example, during a recent snowstorm I took an in-town route because there was no traffic on the smaller roads. The interstates were bumper-to-bumper traffic that was moving at ten miles per hour. I made my decision based on current circumstances.

Similarly, leaders understand that part of preparedness is recognizing and optimizing the impact individual communication tools have on delivering information to colleagues. Effective leaders choose the medium that is most appropriate for the purpose and audience of the communication. Leaders start the communication process by being prepared and willing to use communication strategies and formats best suited to delivering a particular message. Being prepared for effective communication requires using methods and modes—paralleling the trip on in-town roads—but also necessitates modeling effective use of new tools that are analogous to interstate highways.

Being prepared means knowing how to use various media effectively. Communication tools are plentiful and range from conventional approaches to innovative electronic tools. Memos, phone calls, face-to-face meetings, e-mails, blogs, videos, and social networking are methods leaders use to disseminate information. To equip themselves to disseminate information in the most effective manner, leaders research best practices, learn how to use the media, and analyze how others use specific tools. So, just as a GPS is inoperable without a satellite, delivering information is unproductive without preparation.

## SELECTING A MEDIUM

Leaders prepare for communications by assessing the type of news to be related and then determining the best format and method for sharing the information. Audience size, time constraints, policy requirements, and subject matter impact how a leader chooses the best communication tool. Leaders choose a tool based on whether information will be disseminated to a whole group, small group, or to an individual. No matter what the size of the audience, leaders need to decide if a face-to-face meeting would be the best format or if e-mail may be just as effective and appropriate. Time constraints for distributing the information impact the medium chosen, and effective leaders know when to use a meeting format versus an electronic communication because they are responsible for determining whether sending out information immediately is critical. Other criteria a leader must assess prior to communicating a message are its consistency with current policy and its potential for generating an emotional response.

When preparing to communicate, leaders research best practices. Some tools are best used in group settings while others are best suited for one-on-one communications. Effective leaders determine if the message is for internal or external customers and whether the information is time-sensitive. The type of information impacts which tool is best. An aid to selecting communication tools is provided in table 1. Each tool is analyzed through the specific criteria in the table.

Once a tool has been chosen leaders then prepare for disseminating information. In each of the following situations careful preparation is a key to the success of the meeting and communication.

A memo is effective when a leader needs to communicate specific information. Memos are brief and explain a key idea concisely. Ideas in a memo

**Table 1:** Tools are chosen based on the size of the audience, type of recipient, time requirements, and content of the message.

| Tool | Audience Size | Recipient | Time/Priority | Content |
|---|---|---|---|---|
| Memo | Large Group | Internal | Important | Policy or Process |
| Letter | Large Group | External | Important | Information |
| Phone Call | Individual | Internal/ External | Urgent and Important | Information |
| Face-to-Face | Large Group | Internal | Urgent | Policy or Process |
| E-mail | Individual | Internal | Urgent and Important | Information |
| E-mail | Large Group | Internal/ External | Urgent | Policy or Process |
| Blog | Large Group | External | Not Time Sensitive | Need Feedback |
| Video | Large Group | Internal | Important | Information |
| Social Networking | Large Group | External | Immediate | Need Feedback |

stand out because of the laser like description of the subject and purpose of the communication. Often bullet points are used to outline messages and encourage the reader to see and remember key points. Like other communication tools, a memo must be accurate and well organized. The format of a memo assists in focusing the reader on the important information. A memo includes a heading that contains the date, full names and titles of the writer and receiver, and designates a clear-cut subject.

Letters are similar to memos because they are dated and sent to a specific audience from a specific person. Information in a letter is concise yet enables more complete explanation. A leader uses a letter to send information to an audience outside the organization. A letter should begin by stating the purpose of the communication and continue with more detailed paragraphs that anticipate questions surrounding the topic. When communicating an important idea, a policy, or a change in process to people outside of the school a letter is effective.

Phone calls are appropriate when face-to-face meetings are not possible, but necessary. One benefit to a phone call over a written communication is that the leader and recipient hear voice intonation. Tone of voice provides insight into the attitude and emotion of each participant. Additionally, a phone call is sometimes the most appropriate way to deliver confidential information when a leader does not want to leave an electronic footprint.

Calling a large meeting is effective when information must be disseminated to every member of the organization. Having one large meeting saves time and assures that the same message is heard by all. In situations in which new initiatives, policies, or procedures are shared, large meetings allow all to hear the conversation, questions, and concerns. If the topic is an emotion-laden subject, a large meeting provides opportunities for leaders to guide colleagues in discussion during the event. When appropriate preparation occurs, large group meetings are extremely effective because the audience's need for information is balanced with efficient use of time to discuss and answer whole-group questions.

Sending e-mail is quick and useful when information is needed immediately. A leader reviews key points when preparing to send e-mail. The benefit of e-mail is that it provides a date stamp, creating a record of when information was shared. The message reaches all members of the organization at approximately the same time. When the message has little or no emotional component, an e-mail is often the most convenient choice.

Blogs and social media serve different communication purposes for leaders. Both provide opportunities for feedback through comments. Blogs have benefits over social media, as the platform provides an opportunity for more detailed information. A leader can develop an idea more thoroughly when blogging. Links to important information can be embedded into a blog. Blog information develops over time, allowing an ongoing conversation to develop around a topic. On the other hand, social media is more immediate. It is for short messages that may be time sensitive. Social media also provides opportunity for feedback, but the comments on social media are usually short.

Videos still have a place in communications. There are times when a leader is not in the right place at the right time. If information needs to be communicated to colleagues and there is a distance involved leaders can use various forms of video to bring information to a large group. Using video saves time because there is no need for colleagues to travel to retrieve information. When decisions need to be made, a video conference provides opportunity for discussion and resolution of an issue.

One-on-one meetings take preparation as well. Leaders who prepare create an agenda and talking points so all pertinent information is covered. Small meetings are useful when only one person in the organization needs to receive information. An example is when employees are being evaluated. Talking with colleagues one at a time is also effective when each person has different input affecting the outcome of the news, such as when a leader needs to explain downsizing or funding changes. One-on-one meetings are confidential, constructive, and dependent on different variables with each colleague.

## TECHNOLOGY WITH A HUMAN TOUCH

Leaders need to be forward-thinking and prepared to embrace new technologies while adding a humanistic element. A major impact of digital communications is learning how to prepare a message that is personal and incorporates appropriate opportunities for input and social interaction. When getting ready for a trip, depending on technology tools to guide travel is smart. Even GPS units provide a human-like touch to their output through the voice feature. GPS audio technology, though mechanical in tone, is critical to its effectiveness because it enables drivers to watch the road rather than read directions from a screen. If a traveler takes a wrong turn, the GPS voice lets the driver know that the route has been recalculated. After listening to input from colleagues, a leader sometimes needs to change the direction of a communication. By listening to others' comments and adjusting the message, a leader adapts to changing needs. When using technology, leaders who encourage input understand the benefits and need for human interaction.

Successful leaders use forethought when deciding on a communication plan. They carefully choose their media for interaction because it is essential to embrace new tools while maintaining the human element in communication. An effective leader may send a handwritten note to congratulate or thank a colleague. This is a personal and thoughtful expression. That same leader would use e-mail to provide immediate date-stamped delivery of information about a mandatory meeting. This forethought shows that the leader understands that recipients must plan and schedule meetings into their busy days. Turning on e-mail applications' alerts such as "message opened" and "message read" provides confirmation that information has been received. These e-mail tools allow the leader to know who has received the message and who has not.

At times leaders prefer face-to-face meetings in which facial expressions and reactions are part of the interaction. On other occasions, a personalized mass-communication method that supports feedback is suitable. For example, Twitter is used for sending messages outside the organization to community members. Tweeting is fast and easy, and brings information to all those who have accounts. Firefox supports Live Bookmarks that allow one-way communication to constituents who register to receive the bookmarks. Facebook sends out messages and gives others the opportunity to make comments. Google provides a platform for communicating documents, calendar dates, and instant-messaging. Delivering information electronically through social media indicates the leader is aware that colleagues have diverse communication styles. Use of varied approaches shows understanding that colleagues in an organization respond to information differently.

Communication options are almost endless and evolving rapidly. Leaders need to recognize the benefits of each possibility. *Leaders* match the best format with the right message by understanding that technology has advantages but human contact is welcomed in some instances.

## PRACTICE MAKES PERFECT

Emergency planning is essential in schools. Safety drills prepare students and staff for disasters that may be caused by fire, tornado, earthquake, or lockdown incident. Although these drills are mandated by law, they are implemented because it is the responsible thing to do. Practicing for tragedies takes the surprise out of incidents; those involved act instead of reacting to unusual situations. On September 16, 2009, a gunman fired his weapon multiple times at a school campus in my district. The entire school went into lockdown. In spite of the surprise and resulting commotion when the shots were fired, staff and students followed the lockdown procedures. All went well during the two-and-a-half-hour lockdown (Jenks 2009). Practicing drills uncovers strengths and weaknesses in emergency responses.

The positive outcome of the drills and assessments of drills was that when a real crisis occurred personnel followed the plan; as a result, no injuries were sustained and the gunman was apprehended. Being prepared for the unexpected meant that police, school personnel, and students followed a practiced plan.

Assessments after a real incident also help refine the procedures. For example, a flaw in the school district's lockdown procedure was revealed during the lengthy lockdown. A student secured in the library had an urgent need to go to the restroom. What should have been addressed in the procedures was not anticipated. Typically, when lockdown drills are administered they do not last hours. After this incident, a bucket, kitty litter, and toilet paper were added to the emergency materials in every classroom in the school district. That need was not the only thing that surfaced from this incident. When the security team reviewed the procedures in place, the assessment allowed the school officials to determine what worked well and what needed to be changed.

Similarly, effective communication strategies take practice and assessment of results. Leaders build on their current communication skills, assess effectiveness of communication strategies used in the past, and replace ingrained less-effective habits by learning new techniques. Adapting communication methods by incorporating new strategies and tools requires practice. For example, embedding a video into an e-mail allows the leader to send a personal visual message without a face-to-face meeting. Learning how to create the video and then import it into an e-mail takes time and training. However, investing time to learn something new shows colleagues that their leaders embrace innovation, and their actions influence employees to do the same.

Research shows that taking on the role of beginner refocuses the brain so leaders see beyond their own view. As Robert Cooper has explained, it is important to look deeper and see unexpected opportunities so that potentially useful strategies are applied rather than ignored (Cooper 2001, 1779–87). Successful leaders know that learning something new and then practicing it changes attitudes and releases old patterns of behavior.

Embracing new methods available to deliver information and practicing new communication strategies can strengthen the more-creative parts of the brain. Recently, a principal in my district started using Twitter to send messages to students. These messages provide information students need to have instantaneously, such as bus changes and alteration of the schedule. The principal discovered that students responded faster to Tweets than to announcements over the intercom.

Facebook is often used by librarians to share information about upcoming events and to make library announcements. Facebook provides the school community with information about the library program. Leaders who use these tools understand that, by providing communications to students, staff, and community, these choices can be good supplements to the library webpage. The more leaders post to Facebook and tweet on Twitter the better they are able to use these tools effectively. In his blog Brendan Schneider encourages new users of Twitter to make their own accounts and then begin by following others on a personal account. His point is that by participating in the activities on Twitter the learner, in this case the effective leader, is practicing how to use the social media effectively (Schneider 2013).

## FOCUS ON DESTINATION

Electronic navigation units mark destination points. When a user pushes the button to go to a set destination, the GPS immediately calculates the path, distance, and time to get there. All leaders know they are responsible for communicating information that brings specific points home so that goals can be met. Leaders who are prepared reach the point of their communication successfully because they have charted the path carefully. They communicate effectively by researching formats, practicing delivery modes, and analyzing how others use specific media to share information. The end result of each communication is a timely dissemination of information to a targeted audience. This care delivers information so colleagues are able to meet organizational goals. When leaders are prepared, listeners are directed to attainable final destinations. With preparation, leaders understand that they have the power within themselves to provide powerful communication.

## EFFECTIVE PREPARATION

For a recent beach trip, packing the car and starting on time were the result of planning and preparation. I knew when we left the driveway that we could have a great trip. The beach spot was researched, the checklist completed, and the trip mapped out. Preparation provided assurance that the beach trip had every good chance for success. In the context of communication, leaders are confident when they know that they have prepared sufficiently. Leaders prepare by concentrating on the end goal. Then they focus on the purpose of the message and move forward from there.

Once the objective of the message has been determined, a leader compiles material to support the message. A sense of organization comes from careful arrangement and selection of how the message is stated, so that the points develop in a logical order. Sequencing the information and summarizing the talking points underscore the importance of the communication. Good leaders review the intent of the communication and the audience's anticipated reaction to it, and are prepared.

Preparedness goes beyond compiling the message and includes delivering messages with the right tools. Leaders are charged with deciding the most effective tools to present information. Sifting through technology and finding the right tool while inserting a human element into communication allow information to come to the receiver at the most appropriate time.

Communication problems arise when leaders are unprepared. A beach trip without preparation can hamper reaching the destination with the supplies needed to make the vacation relaxing. Distractions and diversions may prevent leaders from achieving the purpose of the message. Preparedness counteracts ambiguity by positively focusing colleagues toward the relevance of the communication.

From athletes to salesmen to librarians, professionals today investigate, practice, and implement communication skills and strategies. Some of these techniques may be traditional and some may be new. When preparing to communicate, school librarians can relate their planning to preparing for a trip. Focusing on the destination, effective leaders map out the content and purpose of the message before meeting with stakeholders. Remembering to use technology without neglecting the interpersonal needs of recipients is like making stops along the travel route so all passengers' basic needs and wants are met. Rehearsing the objectives and goals of the communication ahead of time is similar to creating a checklist to make sure all items are packed. Choosing the best technology is deciding whether to drive on the interstate or use in-town roads.

Leadership of the school library program requires constant communication to administration, staff, students, parents, and the community. The school librarian prepares for each communication by thoughtfully analyzing the message from the perspective of those who will receive the information. For example, budget needs must be communicated to administration at the right time via a memo and with a document of supporting data. A face-to-face meeting is important when communicating changes to policies—especially when the changes might evoke emotional responses in stakeholders. A request for help in running a book fair might be most effective as an e-mail blast followed by personal calls. Informing students of newly purchased resources that can help with a current assignment might require an immediate broadcast announcement with a Tweet or Facebook posting. Each communication from a librarian to constituents must show evidence of preparedness to achieve the desired results.

# LEADERSHIP TIPS RELATED TO PREPARING FOR EFFECTIVE COMMUNICATION

▶ Recognize that personal computers and digital communication changed how and when leaders communicate news, events, and directives.

▶ Use traditional and up-to-date tools appropriately to meet expectations and get information out in a timely manner.

▶ Model appropriate use of methods of communication that increase productivity and performance.

▶ Analyze how others disseminate information by researching best practices and then learning how to use media effectively.

▶ Prepare for communications by assessing the type of news to be related and then determining the best format and medium for sharing the information.

▶ Remember that as leader, you are responsible for determining whether it is critical to send out information immediately.

▶ Create an agenda with talking points so all pertinent information is shared in a face-to-face meeting.

▶ Practice communication strategies by building on current skills and replacing ingrained habits.

▶ Demonstrate your leadership by being prepared to initiate communications and incorporate targeted points into messages.

▶ Use one-on-one meetings when there is a need for constructive and confidential conversations with colleagues.

▶ Sift through technology options and find the right communication tool, yet insert a human element, to allow information to reach the recipient at the most appropriate time and by the most appropriate means.

▶ Achieve the goals of the organization by preparing for communication so that the right information is delivered with the right tools and at the right time.

# Chapter 10
## Clarity

**Leadership questions related to clarity in communication are:**

▶  What strategies lead to clear communication?

▶  How does clarity save time?

▶  Who is impacted by miscommunication?

Leaders know that when communicating information clarity is a necessity. Ambiguous communication sabotages the intention of the message and distorts how colleagues respond. The *Onion* is a weekly publication written by comedic journalists. Their reporting is not meant to provide accuracy but, instead, to amuse readers through distortions of everyday events. However, the format of the writers' communication via print and online gives their humorous text the appearance of authenticity. This authoritative appearance confuses some readers who are not clear about the purpose of the stories published in the *Onion*.

On September 29, 2012, the *Richmond Times-Dispatch* ran online an Associated Press article "Iranian News Agency Picks up Onion Article as Fact." The AP article went on to tell how an Iranian news agency took the *Onion* article in its entirety and republished the story several days after it appeared in the *Onion*. Although the *Onion* article was displayed prominently on Iran's semiofficial website Fars, the information was entirely made-up and unverified. The AP article noted that after several hours the story was taken down from the Fars site.

Other news agencies around the world have been fooled by the *Onion* over the years. For example, in 2002 the *Beijing Evening News* reported about the U.S. Congress wanting more bathrooms and a retractable dome in the Capitol building (Associated Press 2012). One purpose of the *Onion* is to make readers laugh through seemingly real events and circumstances that are anything but accurate. Peter Haise, publisher of the *Onion*, stated in an interview, "I think we're this revenge fantasy for journalists" (Wenner 2002).

The stories about the *Onion* illustrate how misunderstanding the purpose of information leads to loss of credibility. Fars, the Iranian website, was fooled and now readers will have questions about the trustworthiness of their reporting. In our own spheres of influence, if incorrect assumptions are made and the intention of messages misinterpreted, then a leader's communication is ineffective and will produce flawed results. Leaders' communication becomes credible and trustworthy when the purpose of the message is clear.

## APPLYING SKILLS LIBRARIANS ALREADY HAVE

Librarians teach students and colleagues how to identify articles and information from sources like the *Onion* to prepare researchers for inaccuracies. Researching information from sources that are known to be fictitious leads to false conclusions, distortions, and misunderstanding. Librarians encourage students who are researching answers to problems to seek resources and information whose authority and validity can be verified. Clarity in research requires defining the problem, finding facts to support a point of view, and solving the situation in ways that the message of the research is understood.

Clarity in communication is based on these same principals. Effective leaders define the purpose of the message, include support information, and resolve any questions so the information is understood. If colleagues are unsure of what is meant by the leaders' communications, then the fault is the leaders'. Clear communicators express goals, purposes, and expected outcomes in ways that colleagues understand.

Creating clarity of goals, purposes, and outcomes involves providing answers to the questions: "Who?" "What?" "Where?" "When?" and "How?"

Leaders articulate and explain all messages from simple to complex by answering these questions.

## REAL-LIFE EXAMPLES

Journalists use questions to collect and report detailed information to satisfy readers' interest in a particular story. In 2002 the East Coast was dealing with the gripping terror of a series of sniper shootings along the Washington, DC, beltway. Two gunmen were eventually caught after twenty-three days of panic. On the tenth anniversary of the shootings, the *Richmond Times-Dispatch* ran a series of articles about the events that took place (McKelway 2013). These articles examined multiple aspects about the events and followed up on personal stories of those intimately involved with the shootings and search. The articles were a reminder of the incidents leading up to the capture of the assailants. The reflective articles explained the who, what, where, when, and how of the story, linking the print article to timelines and additional online information.

Similarly, leaders include details in communications so that information is placed in context. Timelines are used to provide emphasis, direction, and deadlines. Leaders keep messages succinct and focused by sketching out talking points that answers who, what, where, when and how when preparing to communicate information.

Training and practice on how to talk with the press gave me a formula for communicating messages. The formula is to state your point, support your point with specific evidence, reinforce the point, and end the message by restating the point of the message. An example of this is a communication I sent to my supervisor to explain the effectiveness of the county-wide library book bowl program, modeled on *College Bowl* and other academic quiz shows.

At the time we had a county-wide focus on increasing students' critical-thinking skills. I began by stating that the school library Book Bowl program promotes critical thinking. I followed with support provided by a parent who had explained that Book Bowl made a difference in her son's life because it gave Evan the chance to bring together his celebrated and, well, not-so-celebrated skills for success. His ability to remember details proved an obvious benefit. But his willingness to take a risk, often characterized as impulsiveness, was precisely what he needed to press the buzzer and offer the winning answer. When Evan's mother asked him how he knew the answer when the clue was incomplete, he explained that only two caretakers appeared in any of the thirty books and only one cut grass. I reinforced the idea that Book Bowl participants are provided with practice in fast-paced logical reasoning, practice that benefits them in every class and in life. I concluded with restating that students under the guidance of a librarian practice critical thinking skills when preparing to participate in Book Bowl. This is one example how the library program promotes critical thinking. Using this formula presents information in a brief, succinct manner.

## STRATEGIES FOR CLARITY

Clear communication, especially written communication, is the result of concise wording, placing information in context, and appropriate use of images.

### Concise Wording

Straightforward communication is best understood by travelers who rely on signage to successfully reach their destinations. Airports are known for providing directions with clear signage. The signage has to be clear; if it isn't travelers will falter, miss destinations, and get lost. Short verbiage with directional arrows and images bring clarity to passengers about gate information, navigating various terminals, and locating amenities.

Amsterdam's Schiphol Airport was built before the First World War. In 1960 it was moved and redesigned. The architects asked Benno Wissing to create signage. He came up with a plan that used bright yellow and green illuminated signs. Yellow signs gave directional information for passengers to get to gates and terminals while green signs indicated services. For visibility Wissing increased the size of the font and placed the signs up near the ceiling. He even produced smaller signs using lowercase fonts for secondary information. At the time 12 to 15 percent of airport passengers in other European airports missed their flights while the passengers at Schiphol boarded on time. As a result of these successes airports all over the world adopted Wissing's principles when constructing signage (Bos 2011). Today digital signs provide airport managers with additional ways to deliver immediate information to travelers.

Leaders know when to use print, face-to-face, digital, or a combination of communications to emphasize and ensure clarity when relaying information.

If Benno Wissing's contribution to airport signage is a model for leaders, then communications from leaders need to model Benno Wissing's system. His signs were understood because they were simple, exact, and relevant. Leaders express clarity of goals, purposes, and outcomes by presenting the information in everyday language, with specific details, and in appropriate context of the organization.

## Importance of Context

Various formats of communication demand context. Authors of e-mail messages and any other written communications always run the risk of misinterpretation. Leaders who use written communication need to understand what neuroscientist Robert K. Cooper explains in his book *Get Out of Your Own Way* (2006). In the book he states that the brain doesn't do well with words alone because written communication removes the tenor of a speaker's voice and facial expressions. Cooper notes that 80 percent of human communication is nonverbal. Therefore, leaders must take great care when drafting written communications.

Leaders recognize that others may not read information and construct the meaning the author intended. They know their audience and work to make communication short and free of jargon and inaccuracies. Audiences filter information through knowledge gained from personal and professional experiences. Leaders consider their audiences' prior knowledge when deciding whether or not to use acronyms and job specific phrases. Knowledge of the meanings of professional lingo is dependent on the audiences' ability to make sense out of the linguistics. Several years ago I created a presentation when the county librarian evaluation process was modified. My entire presentation was educational acronyms. I did this to point out the differences between the old evaluation process and the new. The new added a letter to its name so that the evaluation went from being the Professional Growth Plan (PGP) to the Professional Growth and Evaluation Plan (PGEP). The changes to the process were actually more meaningful to the librarians because I used acronyms. For any other audience the presentation was inappropriate. The librarians' prior knowledge combined with new information created the basis for a succinct and understandable communication. Any other audience would have been lost because they would not have had the prior information needed to process the message. I revised the presentation repeatedly before the professional development day to ensure clarity of meaning. Likewise, leaders write their messages and revise them to ensure that the flow of information can be interpreted easily and the authors' messages will be clearly understood by the recipients.

## Power of Visuals

Depending on the intent of the message, adding diagrams to a written communication can provide visual learners with a clearer path to understanding the author's meaning. Infographics are visual representations of information. Pictures and diagrams provide clarity to information that is complex by simplifying large amounts of data. Infographics also provide viewers with opportunities to see patterns and relationships. An example of an infographic is a subway map (Rouse 2012).

If actual visuals are not appropriate, sometimes use of analogies in written communication creates pictures in readers' minds. These mental pictures can link familiar ideas with unfamiliar concepts, and provide deeper meaning to readers' interpretation of text. For example, while trying to explain that the district's Internet bandwidth was limited, I mentioned that, under the current system, data was coming through a straw rather than a fire hose. This wording gave a clear picture of why users were experiencing problems when trying to access information over the Internet. When communicating to colleagues with diverse professional needs, analogies provide verbal pictures of the message in a language that is understood.

An effective analogy places the point that needs to be conveyed in context for the group hearing the message. Librarians pride themselves on leading teachers and students through each instructional day in order to help them reach academic goals. An analogy provided by a group of coaches at my school exemplifies the fact that they considered the librarians to be academic leaders. During a professional development session this group of coaches described the librarian as the quarterback for the academic team guiding teachers to move all students toward the goal of graduation. This analogy gives a clear picture of the importance these coaches placed on the role of the librarian. They viewed the librarian as one who coordinates the instructional efforts of teachers so that students reach graduation. As a result of the coaches' statement I used that analogy with other groups of educators when trying to explain the importance of school librarians. Leadership is placing information in context to provide clarity so the message is well-defined.

## TWO-WAY STREET

Providing a mechanism for feedback and questions is a key to clarity in all written communications. If colleagues have questions, they need to know how to get answers. A successful communicator requests readers (or listeners) to ask questions about a communication. Recently, I sent out a long communication about a grant. I wanted it in writing so that the school librarians would be able to refer back to the processes that needed to be followed for them to spend a large amount of money.

After receiving several inquiries from librarians about the written communication, I sent out a "frequently asked questions" document to help others who might stumble across the same concerns. This follow-up communication served to repeat the critical points while clarifying specific steps in the process. Had I not provided a mechanism for feedback, I may not have realized that clarification was needed.

Metaphors and stories also can serve as tools that are valuable in face-to-face communication where time is fluid and the audience is able to see facial expressions and hear tone of voice. Metaphors compare one idea to another, creating a picture and understanding by referring an unknown to something that is well known. Metaphors and stories create understanding by permitting the listener to reframe the message and interpret difficult information. Leaders who use metaphors allow their colleagues to see something old in something new (Spector 1996). Knowing the meaning of what is being communicated is critical to clarity. In verbal communication leaders create respect and trust by explaining *why* the message is important.

In face-to-face meetings, describing why something is important provides an opportunity for two-way communication, especially when the leader actively seeks feedback, taking time for colleagues to ask questions about points they do not understand. Questions permit leaders to emphasize the message by furnishing explanations that restate key points.

Vince Lombardi stressed that the advantage of repetition was in making sure all recipients get the point of the message. He explained that in football a lesson misunderstood by one person results in a mistake that instantly negates the efforts of ten other people (Lombardi 2002).

Using tools such as repetition, metaphors, and stories transforms everyday announcements into compelling communications. More importantly, leaders who are effective communicators provide colleagues with an opportunity for feedback to ensure that clarity is achieved.

## HAZARDS OF UNCLEAR COMMUNICATION

If a leader is not clear in communications, the result is confusion. Ambiguous communication undermines the focus for recipients because they must waste time trying to figure out what needs to be done. A more disturbing impact of confusing information is that efforts intended to achieve perceived objectives may meet with failure, may be completed incorrectly, or may be counterproductive. Morale is lowered when team members struggle to understand goals and expectations.

The potential causes of miscommunication are many. Words that have multiple meanings demand explanation in both oral and written communication. A disconnect between what is said and what is interpreted causes miscommunication. A study of teachers in the classroom identified specific phrases that have one meaning for teachers but another for students. Phrases like "Are there any questions?" may be an honest attempt by the teacher to ensure students understand. Unfortunately, students perceive this question as closure to a discussion (Simpllico 2002). The teacher hears no questions and interprets that silence as understanding when, in reality, the students have not thought about what was said or monitored their own comprehension.

Leaders create clarity when they consciously avoid vague and misleading words and phrases. By carefully selecting and reflecting on the language in communications, leaders can achieve clarity, resulting in successful interactions between leaders and colleagues.

## DAILY IMPACTS

Opportunities for librarians to communicate important issues happen daily. Communications with administrators, teachers, students, and parents should be clear and meaningful. By incorporating analogies, metaphors, stories, and graphics into messages, leaders can make the information more understandable. Clarity is especially important when communicating budget concerns, scheduling conflicts, or instructional strategies to colleagues.

Most administrators, teachers, and students appreciate information that is succinct because it shows that the school librarian values their time. Library jargon is confusing to people who aren't librarians, so leaders choose to use language that the audience understands. Knowing which tools to use for different audiences is also critical for communicating information about the school library program, its successes, and its needs.

School librarians who are effective leaders use multiple avenues to publicize program goals, purposes, and expected outcomes. Choosing appropriately from traditional communication tools, social media, and other digital tools for oral and written communication indicates that a school librarian understands the audience who is receiving the information. Appropriate use of communications in isolation or in combination is critical to ensuring clear understanding of information.

## LEADERSHIP TIPS RELATED TO CLEAR COMMUNICATION

▶ Recognize that ambiguous communication sabotages delivery of the intended meaning of the message.

▶ Be a clear communicator by expressing goals, purposes, and expected outcomes in ways that colleagues understand.

▶ Create clarity by providing answers to who, what, where, when, and how questions.

▶ Sketch out talking points when preparing to communicate information.

▶ Understand the necessity for concise wording, effective use of images, and placement of information in context.

▶ Prepare to deliver a message with a clear focal point so that listeners are guided to an attainable final destination.

▶ Remember that written communication removes the tenor of a leader's voice and facial expressions; therefore, be sure that written communications can standalone and cannot be misunderstood.

▶ Recognize that others may not interpret information as having the meaning the author intended.

▶ Avoid confusing colleagues; confused recipients ignore the meaning of a communication.

▶ Use analogies, metaphors, and stories to create understanding by permitting listeners to reframe the message to aid in their interpretation of difficult information.

# Chapter 11
## Silence

**Leadership questions related to silence as an aspect of communication are:**

▶ When is silence a communication tool?

▶ How does silence from colleagues impact leadership?

▶ How can the organization benefit from the judicious use of silence?

Silence is a communication tool that occurs in both deliberate and accidental ways. Either instance has a profound impact on the recipient of silences' manifestation. After the attack on the United States on 9/11 the skies went silent. Living in the path of airplane approaches to an airport, I found that silence was accentuated in the days following 9/11. The quiet provided a constant reminder that our country was united with a resolve to overcome adversity.

Sometimes silence indicates that a storm—real or figurative—is on the way. Right before a violent storm the atmosphere often becomes still. This calm before the storm results because warmer air can hold more moisture before condensation occurs (Encyclopaedia Britannica 2012). In history, silence accelerated the dominance of Hitler's Third Reich while hundreds of victims' lives were destroyed. Librarians know that, under some circumstances, silence impedes intellectual freedom.

Silence isn't always an indicator of trouble or disruption, however. The crowd goes silent right before a key field goal in a football game. This silence is in anticipation of the outcome. The silent pause of surprise when receiving notice that an award has been earned lends excitement to the event. In each of these instances silence activates an emotion, a warning, or notice of impending news. Good leaders use silence to punctuate messages knowing that quiet builds anticipation and emphasizes key points.

## WHY EMPLOY SILENCE?

Silence is a necessary tool that lends variety to leaders' communication skills. Leaders who effectively insert silence into communication enhance the message because silence uncovers deep meaning and is refreshing and rejuvenating.. Simon and Garfunkel's song "Sounds of Silence" implies that much that goes on during quiet pauses. They sing about people who talk without speaking, hear without listening, and state that no one dared disturb the sound of silence (Simon 2012). Simon and Garfunkel sing about uncovering deep meaning when they state that people talk without speaking. The silent communication evidenced through actions and body language give insight into what colleagues are thinking and how they are interpreting information. Silence provides a refreshing reprieve when communicating data. Leaders in schools are overwhelmed by data. They hear the data and need silence to interpret data's meaning. If they do not listen to what the numbers are saying they are not able to effectively address student needs. A leader does not disturb the sound of silence when encouraging colleagues to problem solve because in this case silence is rejuvenating and assists critical thinking. In each of these instances silence is powerful because colleagues' attention and reaction to information is improved. In an advertising study silence was proven to enhance attention and recall (Ang, Leong, and Yeo 1999). Successful leaders choose silence as a tool in two-way communication. Perceptive leaders recognize whether silence from colleagues means acceptance of the message or need for more information. If a leader uses silence to provide for reflection, to allow for understanding, to seek opinions, or to assist with negotiations, then the message becomes more meaningful. Leaders know when to use silence and how to interpret silence from colleagues.

## INCLUDING SILENT ELEMENTS IN COMMUNICATION

Leaders can learn some tips about effective communication from silent movies. Silent movies emerged in the late 1800s as entertainment and captivated viewers. Actions and facial expressions were exaggerated to tell a story. Using pictures to convey a concept inserts silence into communication that is entertaining. The entertaining aspect of silent movies captured viewers. But the actors and actresses overstated actions resulted in viewer interpretation. Researching the history of silent films indicates that programs were written and handed out to movie-goers to help tell the story. These programs were important to telling the producers' intended stories. Without words viewers were left to interpret—or misinterpret—meaning behind the storyline.

Silent movies changed the way people expect information. As more people went to silent movies the need for visual cues became more important. Today leaders insert pictures into communication to address colleagues who appreciate receiving visual information.

Pictures included in presentations provide opportunities for reflective thinking and for leaders to emphasize key points silently. Nicholas Carr states that once maps became common people began to picture all sorts of natural and social relationships. (Carr 2010, paragraphs 897-904). Pictures of geographical areas known to people enabled them to understand physical relationships to where they lived. People were then able to make decisions about where to place their homes in relation to markets, water sources, and transportation. A graphic representation of the areas where they lived made a difference to their lives. A graphic in a leader's presentation provides additional information about the message being communicated. Infographics provide colleagues with a means to see relationships between new information and existing knowledge. In addition, viewing the picture gives the leader and his audience time to stop and think quietly about the meaning behind the information.

## FURTHER BENEFITS OF SILENCE

Organizations value innovation, which is dependent on creative thinking and problem solving. Leaders know that silence clears the mind for innovation. It can free the mind of conflicting issues, encourage dialog, and foster creative thinking. The workplace is noisy. Even school librarians proudly comment about organized chaos in the library. Many school librarians state that the library is not a quiet place anymore but, instead, a spot for active learning and sharing. The noise and pace of the day is often seen as a good thing, indicating more human interaction, and signaling progress, energy, and excitement (DiMattia 2005). The quiet calm that used to be is no longer guaranteed.

Progress, energy, and excitement are all good things, but silence is beneficial, too. Silence prevents exhaustion and an over-active mind. Silence opens the way for creativity and innovation by stilling the mind so it can focus on issues and solving problems. Nicholas Carr explains that the development of a well-rounded mind requires both an ability to find, process, and reflect on a wide range of information (Carr 2010, paragraphs 2865-2879). Silence provides important time to still the mind and develop innovative responses to needs. Leaders need silence to develop messages and determine how to communicate them effectively. Listeners need silence sometimes to absorb messages and reflect on them.

## SILENCE AS HINDRANCE

Absence of information is like silence because it creates a gap between what is being said and final expectations. Colin Powell has explained that silence from colleagues hinders knowing what is really happening. An effective leader needs to know how to draw information from colleagues. Leaders encourage colleagues to feel comfortable with saying "I don't know" because honesty with lack of information is better than incomplete or poor data. Colin Powell also cautions that when colleagues insert qualifiers like "my best judgment," "reliable sources say," and "for the most part," then information is not based on verified facts (Powell 2012, 115–16). Leaders know that when colleagues use these qualifiers, valid data may not be available.

Effective questioning allows leaders to sift through the information to determine what is verifiable and what is based only on gut feelings. Colleagues who are questioned effectively by their leader then begin to ask better questions when seeking information. They understand the negative impact of gaps in verifiable information and report back to their leader with honesty.

Due to the potential for incomplete information leaders need to interpret the intent behind reported data before making decisions. On the other hand, when colleagues do not have definitive facts, it is appropriate to ask them to provide an interpretation of events. This process helps leaders filter information before creating solutions and making decisons. Powell states that sometimes a leader does not know what he knows until he finds out what colleagues don't know. Colleagues need to be honest and feel comfortable stating they do not know something (Powell 2012, 115–16).

Leaders who develop a caring and open communication style with colleagues find information is reported truthfully. Through trust, colleagues begin to understand that silence demands seeking better data before reporting to their leader.

## SILENCE TO ENCOURAGE THOUGHT

Leaders understand that colleagues can better interpret information as the result of intentional moments of silence. In the quiet spaces during information dissemination listeners have time to place information into context. Leaders that rush to deliver a message miss the chance to gain insight into how colleagues are interpreting the message. Silence during a presentation or meeting also provides space for people to communicate feedback and state their opinions and feelings. It provides time for the recipients of the message to think, formulate questions, and understand the message.

School librarians know that when asking students questions, pausing to give students time to think results in better answers with more student participation. Professional communication is the same. Pausing gives colleagues an opportunity to ask questions and express points of view. Wait-time after a colleague answers a question or responds to information provides time for others to comment. Leaders also need wait-time to consider comments made by colleagues. During quiet time leaders determine whether the message was understood. Listeners' facial expressions and body-language during wait-time also give leaders insight into how information has been perceived.

## LESSONS FROM SEINFELD

Sometimes nothing, known in math as zero, has tremendous potential. An episode of Jerry Seinfeld's show told the story of when Jerry accepted the NBC network's invitation to meet about developing a new series. In the episode, George suggests they do a series about nothing. The premise was that the show would be based on everyday things rather than a specific character.

Like the premise of *Seinfeld*, silence may seem like nothing, emptiness, and unproductive, but silence needs to be an everyday communication strategy. Silence has potential for bringing out the inner voice of the organization. When leaders become silent coworker's opinions, individual comments, and personal perspectives are given an opportunity to be heard. Leaders know that colleagues' responses help identify corporate thought.

When leaders listen to varied perspectives others feel their opinion is valued. Listening by being silent exhibits a caring side to leadership. Leaders know the outcome of consistently paying attention to coworkers is that the workforce is encouraged to use open dialog. Focusing on "nothing" was a gamble that paid off during season four of *Seinfeld* when the show won the Emmy for outstanding comedy series (Castle Rock 1998). The reason the gamble paid off was because everyday things *are* something. Silence should be an everyday thing. All too often in the busy technology-driven work environment, silence suffers. When silence is not an everyday thing, then communication falters because the organization's inner voice is suppressed. Successful leaders use and interpret silence every day to emphasize relevant and timely information, understand information, seek opinions, and negotiate results.

## SILENCE AS NEGOTIATION TOOL

Every leader ends up in situations that require negotiation. Leaders understand that some of the best negotiating is the result of silence. Although holding back comments is hard, a good negotiator uses silence to force comments from the other person (Gilpatrick 2001). The silence during negotiation also provides thinking time, especially when leaders are boxed into a corner. When leaders are not talking, they are also not making concessions! John Bradley Jackson mentions that it takes practice to be silent. He suggests that negotiators stop talking and occupy the time by taking notes. This is a tactic that provides an opportunity to practice silence while keeping engaged. He also states that silence cues the other side to speak. More importantly, silence can force the other party to state his or her position first, resulting in a strategic advantage for the silent negotiator (2006).

Silence emphasizes that listening is an important component of understanding. As a result of silently waiting, the negotiator also becomes an active listener who attempts to fully understand the information being given. Breaking the silence by restating what the other person has said allows the listener to know if the information heard has been interpreted as the speaker intended.

## IMPORTANCE OF BALANCE

Today librarians battle the stereotype of being known as "shushers" and demanding quiet. Articles abound explaining the need for a balance between noise and quiet. In 2005 the journal *American Libraries* ran an article entitled "Silence is Olden." It described the changing landscape of libraries and how the best solution is to view the library in its entirety, and provide a balance between active areas and quiet sections. The article stated that "a library is a community center, but it's also a place for study; a sanctuary, but a space that encourages active exchange of ideas" (DiMattia 2005).

Some people consider maintaining silence to be part of librarians' inbred skills. Using silence effectively is one choice among many communication tools school librarians may select. It can assist librarians in situations where understanding of another point of view is needed.

For example, if a librarian is introducing a new initiative to the school library program, including silence in the presentation is an effective tactic to obtain colleagues' reaction. Silence gives others time to internalize the idea and respond with meaningful questions. And when librarians use pictures to create silence during a presentation, the strategy encourages feedback, dialog, and creative thinking.

If librarians are in a situation calling for negotiation, practiced silence creates pockets for the other side to speak. Knowing what the other party is thinking enables compromise. Librarians who develop silence as a communication tool know its value in bringing out the organization's inner voice to position library needs for successful acceptance.

## LEADERSHIP TIPS RELATED TO SILENCE
## AS A COMMUNICATION TOOL

► Recognize that good leaders use silence to punctuate messages because quiet builds anticipation and emphasizes key points.

► Use silence to provide for reflection, to allow for understanding, to seek opinions, or to assist with negotiations; as a result, your message becomes more meaningful.

► Create silence by using pictures in a presentation to reinforce a point.

► Be silent to allow an opportunity to listen for understanding.

► Remember that leaders who rush to deliver a message miss the opportunity for important feedback and information.

► Provide wait-time after presenting information so listeners can reflect, formulate questions, and express comments.

► Employ silence to free the mind of issues, encourage dialog, and stimulate creative thinking.

► Allow silence to open the way for creativity and innovation by stilling the mind so it can focus on issues and solving problems.

► Remain silent at times during negotiations to force comments from the other person.

► Listen to make others feel valued and to demonstrate caring.

► Bring out the inner voice of an organization through the sounds of silence.

# Chapter 12

# Results

**Leadership questions related to results and communication are:**

▶ What results are impacted by communication?

▶ Is mentoring part of communication?

▶ How is operational success influenced by communication?

Leaders who produce results communicate with colleagues in ways that motivate action. Just as the jockey is the leader of the team of horse and rider, a leader unites his team, guiding them to accomplish a common goal. As the jockey makes split-second decisions and communicates on multiple levels with his mount, leaders sometimes must make instantaneous judgments on courses of action to guide colleagues through tasks and guide them to the desired end result (Mills 2012). Throughout the race the casual observer notices solidarity between horse and rider. This communion of purpose is vital to the performance and results of the race. The horse and rider become one with a clear goal in mind.

Dr. Jeri Anderson is a chiropractor and an authority on horse racing who has explained that a jockey communicates effectively and effortlessly with the horse without hampering the horse's forward motion. She goes on to describe the relationship between the jockey and horse as one of conservation of energy where just the perfect amount of energy is released at the most opportune moment through that communication (Dorausch 2009). Effective communication by leaders focuses colleagues' efforts so work is accomplished effectively and efficiently. In organizations, communication networks provide results—winning—in timely and productive ways.

Teamwork, mentoring, and tasks are impacted by planned and unplanned communication. A jockey establishes clear, concise communication with the horse to achieve positive end results. The leader, like the jockey, achieves unity by meeting the needs of colleagues under his supervision. A leader delivers communication with clarity, knowing the effect that this clarity has on colleagues' understanding of their job and their role in the operations of the organization. Communication delivered in a confident manner and with clear expectations provides a steadying effect similar to that of a jockey providing a calming touch to the racehorse. The effective leader understands that different employees need different types of communication at different times, and can make that determination on the fly. Effective leaders communicate to individuals and groups through varied communication paths that include digital, written, and oral exchanges.

## COMMUNICATION AND TEAMWORK

Maneuvering the energy level in an organization is dependent on teamwork and communication. Leaders realize the staffing and effort it takes to create and sustain organizational results. To get the horse to the paddock on race day, a team plans how to guide the horse to a win. Breeders, owners, trainers, exercise riders, grooms, and even journalists plot how the horse will go about winning. The process starts with the horse's birth and continues to that moment when the horse is loaded into the starting gate on race day. All members of the horse's team plan how to direct the horse's efforts and determine how to run the race. Often, the team decides to conserve energy at the beginning of the race to initiate a powerful surge at the end of the race, enabling the horse and jockey to cross the finish line first (Mills 2012). The team members share the results of their efforts, celebrating a victory or analyzing the outcomes to determine future training plans.

Similarly, leaders have desired results in mind and communicate information so the team meets objectives in a way that makes best use of colleagues' talents. Leaders anticipate how their communications influence the team to work together to accomplish specific objectives and goals. During the project, information-sharing between the leader and team is constant, enabling work to continue efficiently. When the goal is met leaders evaluate the team's processes and outcomes to determine next steps.

The formation of teams generates a communication network that creates unity when colleagues are focused on a common result. Without teams each person works independently, resulting in inefficient use of people resources, duplication of effort, and, possibly, contradictory and counterproductive work. A leader who focuses on results addresses collaboration to draw colleagues together because the leader knows that teamwork enables each person to achieve significantly more than individual efforts produce in isolation. Robert K. Cooper has related that "deep down the brain is socially wired" and that reality empowers collaboration (2001). Leaders support teamwork and appeal to the social part of the brain by forming committees, task forces, and work groups. The collaborative work of these groups focuses individuals on results that are meeting organizational needs.

Leaders further assist by clearly communicating the purpose, goals, and minimum intended outcomes for the group. Teamwork accomplishes results and enhances understanding by building value and trust. Leaders who urge collaboration appeal to the social side of the brain that thrives on collective energy while working toward professional goals.

One of the first changes I made to the district library program I manage was to develop a system of committees and task forces. These connect librarians within and across grade levels. The teams are charged with a specific set of goals needed to achieve a stronger and more relevant district library program.

When a task force was formed to create an online copyright training program to use as professional development, an elementary librarian explained that the work was fun. She enjoyed working in a group and getting to know the technology teacher at her school and librarians from middle school and high school. Supervising the work of this task force was fun for me as well, yet the key to the task force's success was communication. The task force received information about the purpose of the work as well as minimum intended outcomes. This preparation set up a structure for the group, a structure that focused on results. Members of the group communicated within the group, with copyright authorities outside the group, and with me as they worked toward completing the task force's goals. Each committee and task force in our district unites school librarians and develops a strong bond among colleagues.

## COMMUNICATION AND MENTORING

Mentoring is a one-to-one communication tool that reaps results for the entire organization. Mentors communicate practices, values, and history of the organization to new hires. Leaders see themselves as mentors for colleagues. As mentor, a leader facilitates professional growth by encouraging cross-departmental camaraderie and trust. Just as the jockey becomes mentor for the horse the minute the jockey enters the saddling paddock, the leader assumes a mentoring role from the start. When the jockey meets the horse the jockey is responsible for piloting a victory. The encounter may be the first time the jockey has met the horse, yet he establishes a working partnership, teaching the horse in nonverbal ways how he wants it to behave and respond. The jockey requires a total commitment from the horse, commitment that begins during the warm-up period when there is total give and take between horse and rider. Both horse and jockey communicate specific needs before the actual race, but it is the jockey who guides the horse, making new situations understandable (Mills 2012).

The jockey's demeanor conveys confidence and knowledge to the horse just as mentors express confidence and knowledge to mentees. Building rapport is where the race is won or lost because success is dependent upon trust. Mentoring programs likewise develop professional relationships based on trust between experienced people and new hires. Communication is the foundation of successful mentoring in which mentor and mentee share professional experiences, knowledge, and skills with one another. Forming successful mentoring programs that build on the mission of the organization is the responsibility of the leader. A mentoring program that contains specific content and communication requirements leads to faster assimilation of new hires.

Harvey Homsey has shared that the organization benefits from a mentoring program. He stated that productivity is improved, turnover reduced, and cross-departmental work is encouraged (2010). Both mentor and mentee become sharper as each share their expertise and knowledge. Embedded into the program is a strong communication network that uses e-mail, phone, and face-to-face communication. The mentoring program is a communication tool that provides firsthand information about new hires. In most instances, mentoring of school librarians is remote, meaning that a mentor and a mentee are not in the same building. Usually the library supervisor isn't in the building, either. A mentor is a direct communication link from the new hire to the supervisor, and an extra set of eyes and ears to assist in assessing needs of a new librarian. New hires stay longer and begin contributing faster when they are mentored. The retention rate in my district improved from 56 to 93 percent over a five-year period after instituting a mentoring program.

Another benefit of mentoring programs is that, as new hires and mentors enter the program, more librarians are prepared to assume a leadership role based on their mentoring experience. Collegial communication is deepened and broadened as seasoned mentors assist new mentors and mentees.

## COMMUNICATION AND TASK COMPLETION

Just as the jockey breaks out of the gate and guides the horse through the race and into the last turn, passing fatigued rivals, leaders guide operational success through motivating communication that directly influences the completion of tasks. As the energy level of the straining horse becomes depleted, it is the responsibility of the jockey to communicate his or her strength through hands on the reins and body, instilling confidence in the mount and commitment to the team to accomplish the win (Mills 2012). Leaders also have the ability to motivate colleagues by instilling confidence and an intrinsic desire to follow through on organizational goals.

Essential to completing goals is choosing the best people to complete tasks and then communicating needs to specific members of the organization. Reaching out to them to solve problems shows the leader knows the people who make up the organization.

Astute leaders teach their staff the importance of recognizing when communication cannot wait. Leaders understand the premise that what they do not know will cause problems and hinder success of the organization. Colin Powell has written that when he was working with his staff he let them know that if they saw something that triggered the reaction, "Umm, Sarge, do you think we should call someone?" the answer is always "Yes, and five minutes ago" (Powell 2012, 121).

Colleagues who trust their leaders will communicate news so that the leader has time to be proactive in addressing concerns. Like the jockey who guides the horse through the gate, into the turns, and down the straight-a-way to the finish line, leaders build a trusting environment where communication flows through the organization enabling successful completion of goals.

Leaders share results with the public. Communicating value of the organization to the community promotes understanding. At the end of any horse race, the results of the competition are shared with the viewers via an electronic tote board and through the announcer. The results are judged official, and a time and photo verify the results of the combined hard work of the equine team (Mills 2012). The tradition of the jockey trotting the horse to the winner's circle is appreciated by the viewers in the stands because the act demonstrates the importance of success.

Leaders understand the strategic nature of public relations and create an organized structure to communicate positive information to the community. Just as information about the horse is analyzed and promoted after the win, collecting data about completion of tasks and achievement of goals creates effective reinforcement of the organization's success. Leaders acquire data by evaluating results and analyzing supporting statistics. Data is important to results because it highlights the organization's strengths and weaknesses. Leaders use both positive and negative information to develop the organizational plan and implement changes. The rationale for the changes is clearly communicated to team members. Then as each incremental improvement is achieved leaders share new information with the public.

## COMMUNICATION ABOUT POSITIVE RESULTS LEADS TO FURTHER SUCCESSES

Librarians know that communication within the organization achieves successful results through teamwork and collegial ownership in school library program goals. School librarians who are leaders recognize the value of mentoring and serve as mentors for colleagues. They mentor staff on technology use, collaborative planning, and student self-assessment strategies.

Leaders also understand the importance of communicating results to the public. Communicating results is an essential part of any library promotion plan. Part of that plan is communicating data that proves library successes to those outside the library walls. When parents and community members have this information, they speak up in a knowledgeable way and explain how the school library program contributes to student success and district educational goals. Librarians also communicate results to motivate constituents to action and to develop supportive teams. Just as the jockey leads his horse to victory, the librarian leads the school library program to noteworthy results through teaming and ongoing communication.

## Leadership Tips Related to Communication and Achieving Results

▶ Remember that effective communication networks provide winning results in timely and productive ways.

▶ Deliver messages in a confident manner and with clear expectations to provide a steadying effect similar to that of a jockey providing a calming touch to a racehorse.

▶ Sustain the energy level in an organization by means of teamwork.

▶ Share results of their efforts with team members, celebrating victories and analyzing outcomes to determine future training plans.

▶ Form teams to generate a communication network that creates unity because colleagues are focused on a common result.

▶ Urge collaboration to appeal to the social side of colleagues' brains that is dependent upon collective energy working toward professional goals.

▶ Create mentorships as a means of communicating practices, values, and history of the organization to new hires.

▶ Choose the best people to complete tasks and communicate team members' roles in achieving goals.

▶ Communicate to the community the value of the organization, promoting understanding of program goals, successes, and needs.

▶ Communicate results as an essential part of any library promotion plan.

# Section 4
# Follow the Leader

**RESPONSIBILITIES**

From games of small children to rock music, the idea behind following the leader illustrates that the leader has responsibility to guide the group to a destination. Walt Disney Productions inserted a lively song into the movie *Peter Pan* at the point where the lost boys and the Darling children all follow John as they go off to fight the Indians. Rock music today has many versions of "Follow the Leader."

When my children were growing up I told them that I needed them to be leaders. Because I wanted them to accept responsibility for their own decisions, I told them that I did not care what others did; I wanted others to follow my children, not the other way around. The game of hide and seek inevitably begins with younger children following the older ones to safe spots. After a while, the younger children realize that because of their size they have many opportunities to hide in unique places. The smaller children then take responsibility for their own destinies. A good leader guides followers to the point where followers can then assume more responsibility for their own future.

Accepting responsibility is a major requirement of a leader. Leadership is assuming ownership for developing a vision, empowering others, reaching decisions, and acknowledging excellence.

# Chapter 13

# Visioning

**Leadership questions related to visioning are:**

▶ What does an organization's vision contain?

▶ Where does organizational vision come from?

▶ How do librarians articulate vision for the future library?

Leaders are responsible for providing insight into the future direction of their organizations. Providing this insight is accomplished through a vision statement. Vision statements, like the future, seem like air: hard to grasp and see, but essential. In *Reframing Organizations: Artistry, Choice, and Leadership* the authors' state that "vision turns an organization's core ideology, or sense of purpose, into an image of the future" (Bolman and Deal 2011).

Creating a mental image of a concept is much like interpreting an illusion. Optical illusions make viewers question what they are seeing because illusions distort pictures. Astute leaders are aware that colleagues' interpretations of an organization's vision are much like optical illusions because individual impressions direct understanding of abstract ideas. Leaders make organizational connections to the vision because leaders are responsible for answering the question, "What does the vision statement mean?" Some colleagues need a technical explanation; others accept it for what it is, and others combine the technical and obvious to draw conclusions. Still others read a vision statement and put their own creative touch to it.

## COMMUNICATION OF VISION

Once colleagues form an impression of the vision—even if the perception is wrong—they find it difficult to see the vision any other way. Leaders clarify vision statements so colleagues are able to set direction for future actions. Ultimately, leaders ensure that everyone understands that applying the principles embodied in the vision statement is the organization's ultimate goal.

President Ronald Reagan was known as a man who conveyed his vision to the American public with finesse. He was not known for being a strategist. His success was a consequence of providing vision and then appointing strong advisors known for developing strategic direction (Bolman and Deal 2011). Leaders direct colleagues on the path to implementing the mission and vision of the organization. They do this by removing obstacles created by competing voices based on varied interpretations among colleagues.

Using face-to-face and electronic meetings, leaders initiate conversations to sort through individuals' understanding of the vision. Leaders collect information from these meetings to simplify and order data detailing organizational confusion. Next, they place colleagues' individual experiences into context of the vision so that understanding is achieved.

## ACTIONS FOLLOWING VISION

Once understanding has been accomplished, leaders develop a strategy to convey the clarified vision and prepare for effective implementation. Lee G. Bolman and Terrence E. Deal have stated that "vision without strategy remains an illusion" (2008). Leaders need to bring into focus the fuzzy view of a vision, enabling cohesiveness and meaning to form the basis for an organization to proceed.

Typically, an action plan evolves from a vision statement. An action plan may have multiple goals with interim objectives to implement. Leaders with assistance of members in the organization create a plan for each objective under each goal. Leaders set a timeline for completion of each goal. A vision's effectiveness depends on leaders' assuming responsibility for implementing a strategic plan.

## SCHOOL LIBRARIANS' VISION

In 2007 and 2009 the American Association of School Librarians (AASL) promulgated a vision to guide school librarians and school library programs into the future. The AASL's *Standards for the 21st-Century Learner* and *Empowering Learners: Guidelines for School Library Programs* contain principles to guide school library programs designed to address future needs of learners and school libraries. The learning standards set a new direction for instruction. No longer are school librarians focusing solely on information literacy; instead, librarians support students as they expand information-seeking to encompass multiple literacies.

The students learning under these standards are to be "active and creative locators, evaluators, and users of information to solve problems and satisfy their own curiosity," but librarians must go further than helping students develop these skills (AASL and AECT 1998, 2). School librarians are to focus on developing student dispositions that enable responsible self-assessment of learning and information seeking. The learning standards and program guidelines were constructed with feedback from school librarians across the country. The responsibility for communicating these goals to the members of the organization fell on the leadership of AASL.

When the standards and guidelines emerged, school librarians needed clarity and direction. AASL created a plan to provide strategic direction for implementation of the new vision. The plan, Learning4Life, was constructed to create a shared vision among school librarians. This plan contained a timeline for implementation and addressed librarians' concerns, as well as political and operational issues. Librarians required training on how to use and develop instructional and program strategies; they also needed to be able to verbalize and explain the new vision to their administrators, and school librarians wanted to use the operational structure of the new standards to implement the changes within their buildings.

AASL began with a strong image to symbolize the changes. The phrase

"Learning4Life" and a symbolic representation "L4L" were used to create a simple brand loaded with meaning. Providing all members of the school community with resources and methods to actualize learning for life is the librarians' vision. The number four reflects the four learning standards and the four strands within each standard. AASL focused on four words: think, create, share, and grow. Each word identifies the main concept for one of the four standards. The Learning4Life plan is comprehensive and includes communication and training objectives that encompass local and global implementation strategies. AASL developed a vision and then took responsibility for communicating that vision to the school library community. The Learning4Life plan articulates the vision with clear and comprehensive strategic direction (AASL 2008).

## LEADERS' RESPONSIBILITIES AND IMPACTS

Leaders create visions that revitalize their organizations. They are responsible for balancing the long-term interests of internal and external forces. Rick Newman wrote an article comparing Steve Jobs's vision with the visions of other American business leaders such as Benjamin Franklin, Henry Ford, and Thomas Edison. Newman credited Benjamin Franklin with forming the philosophy of the American middle class. Henry Ford was credited with bringing transportation to all individuals through his mass-produced cars. Thomas Edison was credited with creating sweeping changes to society as a result of developing a lighting system and many other inventions that affected everyday lives of ordinary people. Steve Jobs's major contribution was as a designer, marketer, and technologist who made digital interfaces user-friendly (2011).

Each of these leaders developed visionary ideas based on what society and individual people needed. Within the United States and the global community, the middle class benefited from each invention. Intentionally or not, the future of the middle class was drastically changed as a result of these leaders. Their visions created a culture infused with purpose and resolve because these men addressed needs and challenges by inspiring hope and creative exploration. Many of our daily needs are still met by the inventiveness of Franklin, Ford, Edison, and Jobs. As new materials and resources are found, new variations of products are based on these men's creations. Their collective vision continues to generate inspiration and innovation around the world.

## REAL-LIFE EXAMPLES

Leaders inspire and energize organizations through visioning that keeps the organizations vital. Visionary leaders understand that, to stay relevant and valued, organizations must adapt to societal changes. Ted Turner created Turner Broadcasting System (TBS), a television system that provided broadcasting via satellite to cable networks. Soon after, he launched Cable News Network (CNN), the first around-the-clock television news network ("Ted Turner" 2011). Ted Turner's vision changed the television industry. Today computers and digital devices deliver news immediately to users. This new paradigm for news gathering and dissemination means that changes to the television and newspaper industry are occurring as well. Leaders know that the vision of their organization must reflect change or their product will no longer be used.

Similarly, librarians are faced with the challenge of updating best practices as technologies and expectations evolve. Educational initiatives create change where former practices and programs must be adjusted to prevent obsolescence. School librarians who are visionaries lead their school library programs through educational changes. When state and national assessment measures dictated teacher evaluation and in turn whether a teacher's contract would be renewed, the library program needed to change. Teachers feared for their jobs and became focused on drilling students on specific information that was covered by the end of year and standards of learning tests. Immediately teachers stopped coming to the library because they felt there was not enough time for projects. For the library to be embedded into the school culture, school librarians needed to create new avenues for access and relevance due to teachers' altered perceptions of instructional time.

One solution I instituted in response to teachers not bringing students to the library was a lunch-time program. The programs were relevant to students' interests and connected to curriculum content. For example, programs focused on the Vietnam War, science of deep sea diving, physics of magic, theater monologs, and art. Teachers offered extra credit to those who attended. Each program was repeated during multiple lunches and brought students, teachers, and administrators into the school library. Collaborative opportunities expanded as teachers spent their lunchtime in the library. As a result, teachers began scheduling class time in the library.

The vision I had was to reawaken stakeholders' awareness of the library program's and resources' value to students and staff by meeting their needs in a different way. Another change I instituted was training teachers on how to use the library for shorter projects. By instituting fifteen-minute lessons I discovered that teachers were more willing to give up in-class time. Eventually, teachers began booking longer time in the library where students completed work that was relevant to their information needs and the curriculum.

When standard practices change in the school, librarians are responsible for envisioning adjustments to the library program to meet new needs. As Kate Rix has explained, a "funny thing seems to be happening on the way to extinction." She went on to note that the savviest districts and librarians are remaking the position, taking resources to the classroom, integrating library practices into curriculum, and implementing flexible scheduling for instructional classes (2012).

## FOCUS ON THE FUTURE

Visioning is turning organizations' core purpose into an image of the future. School librarians are charged with instructing learners on how to seek, locate, and use information. In the mission for school libraries, AASL states that the school library program's purpose is "to ensure that students and staff are effective users of ideas and information" (AASL 2009, 8). In envisioning the future, school librarians who position this purpose as a means for answering 21st-century needs will reaffirm the relevance of their program's vision.

In the twenty-first century, a vision for how to ignite creativity is needed as much as in previous times when Benjamin Franklin, Henry Ford, Thomas Edison, and Steve Jobs sparked waves of innovation. Creativity and innovation are dependent on learners who use information to solve problems. Delia Newman has posed a thoughtful question about information seeking. She asked, "What is creativity if not the use of information in new ways?" She went on to explain the importance of critical thinking to analysis of information and application of information to resolving dilemmas (2012, 28). Her insight that learning is grounded in information use is critical for librarians to consider when visioning the future success of school library programs.

## LEADERSHIP TIPS RELATED TO VISIONING

▶ Use vision statements to clarify and set direction for the organization's future.

▶ Make sure all stakeholders know that applying the principles embodied in a vision statement is the organization's ultimate goal.

▶ Update visions to revitalize an organization.

▶ Remember that visionaries create organizations that address needs and challenges by inspiring hope and creative exploration.

▶ Recognize that visionary leaders help organizations adapt to societal changes to stay relevant and valued.

▶ Create new avenues for access, embedding the library into the school culture.

▶ Lead your library programs through educational changes.

▶ Create a vision that turns your organization's core purpose into an image of the future.

▶ Remember that creativity and innovation are dependent on learners who use information to solve problems; foster that creativity and innovation through your library program.

▶ Focus on the idea that learning is grounded in information use; this reality is critical for librarians to consider when visioning the future success of school library programs and their students.

# Chapter 14

# Empowering

**Leadership questions related to empowerment are:**

▶ How do empowering leaders delegate responsibility?

▶ When does coaching and counseling impact empowerment?

▶ What must a school librarian do to become an empowering leader?

Transforming students into empowered learners is a leadership skill. "The term 'transformational' stems from the ability to inspire and develop people as resources and move them to a higher state of existence, transforming them in the process" (Bromley and Kirschner-Bromley 2007). Empowerment is one approach to transforming students into effective learners. Librarians scaffold student learning by giving learners increasing responsibility for applying skills as the developmental needs of learners advance.

Leaders who empower others also seek to advance colleagues into leadership roles by sharing responsibility. Delegating this responsibility in progressive waves of accountability is essential to support colleagues' growth. "Empowering leadership" is defined as those behaviors where power is shared with subordinates and results in raising their level of intrinsic motivation (Srivastava, Bartol, and Locke 2006). If leaders give colleagues too much responsibility too soon, they are set up for failure. If leaders do not share enough responsibility, the result is boredom because repetition kills a risk-taking spirit.

Robert K. Cooper states that "every day you can learn something more about who you are and all the potential that's hidden inside you" (2001, xiv). Leaders tap into that inner curiosity and unleash skills waiting to be used. They do this by taking into consideration developmental phases in colleagues' professional growth. These phases often are associated with behavioral skills as they relate to responsibility, caring, risk taking, and independence. Leaders choose people who understand the objectives and the specific expectations required to accomplish a goal. And they look for people who understand the work environment and are able to accomplish results that combine the objectives of the task with the goals of the organization. Empowering leadership is built around four cornerstones of trust, confidence, expectation, and independence.

## TRUST, CARE, AND UNDERSTANDING

Relinquishing control is important to leadership that empowers others. Leaders who trust, understand, and care for their colleagues are able to release this control. A controlling leader is like a tangled necklace. The key to untangling knotted chains is to loosen the strain on the knot until it opens up. A leader who empowers loosens control so colleagues are free to accomplish tasks. Like a knotted necklace that is pulled too tight to allow the knots to be released, a leader who exerts too much control makes empowerment of others impossible. More control means less creativity and less shared decision making is achieved. Leaders need to trust others.

The reason trust is important to empowerment is because leaders that release control over tasks permit colleagues to creatively and freely solve problems. Leaders begin by trusting their own instincts and later extend trust outward to colleagues. Robert K. Cooper states that two conditions, care and understanding, need to exist for leaders to trust others. Leaders must feel that colleagues understand them. Part of understanding is that colleagues know what matters to leaders. In addition, leaders need to feel that colleagues care about them and make decisions that reflect their needs, interests, and concerns (2001, 47).

The way to accomplish trust through understanding and caring is to notice what truly matters to others. Caring and understanding are reciprocal. In organizations where leaders express care and understanding for colleagues, people reflect that care and understanding back to the leader. Reciprocal care and understanding create deeper meaning to organizational work. Tasks become more important because they fill a need that is critical to individuals in the organization.

The purpose of organizational goals becomes relevant when colleagues are concerned about the impact each task and action has on individuals in the organization. "Caring implies a continuous search for competence. We want to do our very best for the objects of our care" (Noddings 1995, 24). An empowering leader not only needs to be understood and cared for but, in turn, needs to model caring. Nel Noddings has suggested that caring needs to be taught and that caring is a learned process. In the library, "care is a reciprocal relationship beginning with observant school librarians who respond to students' information, reading, learning, and relational needs" (Jones 2012, 7).

Trust, care, and understanding are interrelated dispositions that foster empowerment. For leaders these dispositions permit colleagues to accomplish organizational goals. For librarians trust, care, and understanding foster independent learners.

## CONFIDENCE

Empowering leaders create confidence in learners and in other educators by conducting training and supplying materials needed to complete defined tasks. In the book *Lincoln on Leadership* Donald T. Phillips stated that when Abraham Lincoln took office the country had an "inefficient, poorly trained, and poorly equipped army" (1992, 169). Lincoln went on to identify and train leaders who implemented life and death decisions in spite of the fact that the equipment they used was limited and in worn condition. Lincoln understood that his military leaders were given tasks requiring them to take calculated risks. Risk taking develops endurance, persistence, confidence, and resiliency. He needed leaders who were willing to take risks and assume responsibilities during extremely difficult times.

## EXPECTATIONS

Lincoln selected available personnel and developed them into leaders; he *expected* them to become leaders, and they did. He empowered them while providing them with his support during difficult times. Empowering leadership means providing colleagues with the information and support they need to accomplish tasks and then have confidence in the work they produce. Donald T. Phillips expressed the importance of giving "followers all the support you can, and act on the presumption that they will do the best they can with what you give them" (1992, 136). This assumption that colleagues' performance rises to meet a need in spite of available tools is based on principles of transformative leadership.

Transforming leaders seek to satisfy colleagues' inner needs and drives by engaging them in meaningful tasks (Stahl 1998). Embedding the library into the culture of the school is a task that school librarians control. They provide members of the school community with resources and tools to meet personal and professional demands. By meeting users' needs librarians create a schoolwide attitude that values the school library program.

During Lincoln's presidency the best available equipment was not as robust as he wanted. School librarians deal with that concern as well, yet they motivate learners to accomplish goals by supporting intrinsic informational goals. Empowering librarians create confident learners by preparing them to think critically, research skillfully, read voraciously, and ethically use information (AASL 2009). When librarians fulfill users' information needs and their intrinsic drive for independence, the outcome is a strong conviction that the school library program is valuable—because it is!

## INDEPENDENCE

Colleagues are committed to an organization when they are integral to accomplishing assigned outcomes and goals. Empowerment requires coaching and counseling so that colleagues master the skill of independence (Phillips 1992, 136). Part of coaching is ensuring that colleagues feel free to ask questions of leaders and know that comments will not be judged. An empowering leader guides colleagues toward independence by using series of questions, prompting colleagues to evaluate possible solutions to issues. Coaching or counseling via a two-way dialog requires leaders to remain neutral on issues so that all ideas have a fair opportunity for evaluation (Goldsmith 2007).

Not long after I became supervisor of the district library program a concern surrounding the future direction of a Book Bowl reading incentive program arose. This program is a battle-of-the-books-style event in which teams of fifth-graders compete by answering questions about thirty books. Eventually, two teams emerge to compete in the final round. Librarians formed differing views of how the future of Book Bowl should evolve. Each side was strongly opinionated on the solution.

I spent time gathering information on the details of each group's concerns. One wanted to expand the program, while the other wanted to maintain the integrity and rigor of the program. The expansion group preferred to allow more teams to compete and was insisting on a process of triple elimination. Due to time and space constraints, holding the expanded competition in one day seemed unrealistic. The group wanting rigor could not see how the integrity of producing a final round with the two top teams could be maintained with a larger number of teams competing over a longer period of time.

I brought both groups together to meet. Knowing their concerns, I approached the meeting with solutions that addressed their concerns. First, I found a larger facility that enabled eight teams to compete at the same time; as a result, the event could start and finish in a single day. As each side presented their concerns I presented them with options. They discussed the options and agreed on a solution. By the end of the meeting both groups had come together and were united on how Book Bowl would proceed. A triple elimination, more teams, and maintaining the integrity of the results were all do-able. Both sides left the meeting excited about the new plan.

In this situation, I provided logical and realistic options, but the committee members decided on the solution. Monitoring my responses to maintain a neutral stance was essential for empowerment. Not giving them the answer but giving them possibilities empowered each group to expand their views. Each person on that committee went on to use empowerment skills as they continued to work through changes in the Book Bowl program.

## APPLYING SKILLS LIBRARIANS ALREADY HAVE

School librarians already use these same strategies when working with learners on projects. They know that doing the project for the learner creates dependency. As a result, librarians empower their learners with options. The learners then decide how to proceed with these options. Paralleling this approach to developing students' independence as leaders, an empowering leader provides colleagues with necessary authority, resources, and independence.

An expectation of empowerment is leadership development. School librarians empower learners who become leaders of their information-seeking. The title of the national guidelines for school library programs published by AASL uses the word "empowering" in its title. The expectation is that librarians will lead school library programs that empower learners to be accomplished, successful, citizens.

The vision of the school librarian is one of delegating information-seeking responsibility in increasing levels of accountability. As students' skills mature, librarians coach and counsel them to reflect upon their learning by using a two-way dialog that develops independence. Through exploration and discovery librarians raise students' level of intrinsic motivation. An essential goal of empowerment is for librarians to provide support and tools that encourage students to take leadership of their own learning.

School librarians' model caring that generates unshakable competence. The resulting confidence enables students to trust their own ideas and others' ideas. Sharing motivates them to meet higher expectations and develops independence. When students take responsibility and leadership of their own learning, empowerment is achieved. School librarians can use the same process to empower colleagues.

## LEADERSHIP TIPS RELATED TO EMPOWERING OTHERS

▶ Empower others by delegating responsibility in progressive waves of accountability.

▶ Remember that if leaders give colleagues too much responsibility too soon, the colleagues are set up for failure.

▶ Relinquish control when others are ready to assume responsibility.

▶ Recognize that the more control the leader exerts the less creativity and shared decision making is achieved.

▶ Begin by trusting your own instincts and later extend trust outward to colleagues.

▶ Model and foster reciprocal care and understanding to create deeper meaning to organizational work.

▶ Empower others by recognizing the need to provide deadlines, training, and materials needed by others to complete defined tasks.

▶ Provide colleagues with information and support to accomplish tasks with confidence.

▶ Encourage the two-way dialog essential to coaching and counseling.

▶ Provide colleagues with the necessary authority, resources, and independence.

# Chapter 15

# Decision Making

**Leadership questions related to decision making are:**

▶ Who is responsible for making organizational decisions?

▶ Are there group responsibilities in decision making?

▶ What are the impacts of bad decisions?

Leaders are responsible for making decisions. That is their job. On his desk President Truman had a sign with the phrase, "The Buck Stops Here" (Harry S. Truman Library and Museum n.d.). During his presidency his decisive decision making strengthened the office of the presidency. He was responsible for rulings that set policy for future actions by the United States. During his administration the policy of "Containment" of Communism established the attitude of the United States toward the cold war for decades. He created the Central Intelligence Agency, was instrumental in the decision to drop the bomb on Hiroshima, and was concerned about Civil Rights issues (Bowker 1998). Truman stated, "The President—whoever he is—has to decide. He can't pass the buck to anybody. No one else can do the deciding for him. That's his job" (Harry S. Truman Library and Museum n.d.). At the end of the day, leaders are responsible for making, implementing, and being accountable for decisions that are made.

Decision making comes in many styles, and each carries specific responsibilities for leaders. Military leaders use the chain of command in which everyone has a defined responsibility, culminating in a final decision. Secret decision making is used by self-organizing units where "communication between top leadership and local units moves through a clandestine labyrinth of secret couriers and codes" (Bolman and Deal 2008). Consensus decision making relies on plans that reflect the best idea of a group. Shared decision making, which is effective in most schools, requires high-level involvement and high performance from colleagues in the organization. A responsibility of leaders is to direct collaborative efforts and energy toward development of an organization in which decision making is shared. No matter what style leaders employ, they are responsible for reaching a decision and then being accountable for the results of ensuing actions.

## LETTING GO

Shared decision making involves leaders who are responsible for developing colleagues into decision makers. Shared decision making requires leaders to relinquish control. Daniel Pink has suggested three steps for leaders to use to let go of control. First, for colleagues to become engaged in the vision of the organization, leaders need to bring colleagues into goal-setting conversations. When colleagues are essential to goal setting they are more likely to have ownership in their completion. Second, Pink cautions leaders to refrain from using the words "must" or "should." Instead, using the word "consider" enables leaders to express ideas without their sounding like a command. And Pink concludes with advising leaders to let colleagues come to them. Experience shows that colleagues will seek advice when they reach a stopping point or a place where someone with a global vision is needed (2009).

## POWER OF GROUPS

Leaders know that the shared decision-making process is more than making decisions. It requires gathering groups together who are decision makers. Groups must have the "ability to develop better alternatives, rank the alternatives that are developed, make better group decisions even in contentious environments, and sell or defend decisions successfully within any organizational hierarchy" (Safi and Burrell 2007). Leaders who understand shared decision making know that their guidance as groups develop is important. Task forces and committees are avenues for school librarians to encourage shared decision making within the school environment. As school library programs and needs surface, responsible librarians use the format of shared decision making to create open dialog and an environment of inclusiveness.

## APPLYING SKILLS LIBRARIANS ALREADY HAVE

Decision making is dependent on critical thinking and problem solving. Every decision from the smallest to the largest relies on these two skills. Leaders manage decisions by implementing critical-thinking skills and problem-solving skills, with the understanding that solutions often have far-reaching impact on colleagues and the direction of the organization.

School librarians already emphasize the importance of critical thinking and problem solving to learners. One of the effective practices for inquiry is "stimulating critical thinking through the use of learning activities that involve application, analysis, evaluation, and creativity" (AASL 2009). When students seek answers to questions, relevance is important to ensure that they internalize the inquiry process. In addition, each learning task that students undertake builds on previous learning experiences. School librarians lead students through the research process by providing a variety of information resources. Students ultimately make the decision about which resources they will pursue in the information-seeking process. After locating information, learners analyze the data and evaluate what is important to answering their inquiry question. Innovative and creative solutions to their original question are evident in the final student product. Any inquiry process that incorporates strategies associated with critical thinking and problem solving guides leaders and students through a thoughtful decision-making process.

Critical thinking is sifting through confusing information to find important data. A leader who is a "critical thinker is able to distinguish high-quality, well-supported arguments from arguments with flaws, poor data, or weak evidence" (Safi and Burrell 2007, 3).

Colin Powell has related an incident in which he was reporting to a congressional committee. Senator Waxman, who served on this committee, challenged Powell's information. When Powell went back to his team to determine the accuracy of the data, he found that the report contained errors in categorization and counting of terrorist activity. Reliance on this inaccurate data then resulted in flawed decision making (Powell 2011).

Somewhere, in the process of analyzing data, questions must address how information is collected and reported. Leaders must be skeptics and ask probing questions when information related to an expected decision is provided. Leaders should analyze the evidence to determine if any bias has influenced compilation of the report (Mason 2007). Leaders must also reconstruct the information within the framework of the requested need. At that point a final decision can be made based on accurate information and data.

## LACK OF DECISION

Not making a decision often causes bad decisions to occur to fill the void. Failure to make a decision creates instability and confusion. When decisions are delayed or not forthcoming, distorted timelines jeopardize completion of goals. When a decision is needed, someone or some project is stalled and needs a leader's guidance.

I once worked for a principal did not take responsibility for making decisions. As a result, when committees requested confirmation or direction, getting his input was difficult. This situation was frustrating for committees because solutions and actions developed by the committees were well thought out. Although the committees were ready to move forward, deadlines would pass and still the principal had not weighed in on suggested resolutions. This principal was unresponsive when prompted for an overdue decision.

As chair of a committee, I remember feeling uneasy about going ahead without the principal's insight. However, I had only two choices: I could continue with the group's decision, or I could trash the committee's hard work and do nothing. Since I was responsible for many projects under this administrator, I just moved forward, and the results were always positive. When I reached the point where the principal's input in the decision-making process was desired but not available, I spent time reflecting back and analyzing the steps taken by the team to that point. The committee's use of critical thinking and collaboration reinforced my confidence in the members' work. This review provided me with a check on the committee's proposal, and I would proceed ahead unless there was a need for a moral or ethical decision from the principal. In each instance no decision would have stopped progress for the school, and the outcome would have negatively impacted students and staff.

Understanding the principal's motives or underlying rationale for declining input is not important. What is important is that leaders are responsible for making decisions. In this case I developed leadership skills of decision making and the risk taking involved with each decision for which I proceeded forward without administrative review. Librarians do need to understand that schools are political entities, and lack of decision making on the part of the principal may be a direct result of the fact that responsibility, accountability, and blame are attached to any decision that is not successful (Safi and Burrell 2007). Responsible leaders move beyond worry of negative results. They base sound decisions on critical thinking strategies and move the organization toward its goals.

## REMOVAL OF EMOTION

Problem solving is the companion to critical thinking. "Leaders need to be the spark that ignites problem solving in their people rather than assuming they can problem solve alone" (Kerfoot 2011, 290). Leaders take responsibility for problem solving by forming groups to determine root causes of issues and identify effects related to each cause. Problem solving tools such as a fishbone diagram, which is a type of mind map, are available to determine cause and effect (Tague 2004). When leaders use well-constructed tools for problem solving, they take emotion out of the equation and provide a process for solving issues.

For example, when a school library has lower circulation one month, the librarian often looks for causes for the decrease. After determining several factors, such as the number of days the school was open that month and the number of assemblies that occurred during the month, one cause may stand out as having a significant impact on circulation. In one library I managed, standardized testing was held in the library five days during the month, effectively closing the library for circulation. The essential question to solve was, "Can circulation increase when the library is closed for testing?"

Using a fishbone cause-and-effect tool, the identified problem is filtered through existing policies, procedures, people, and machinery that impact circulation during standardized testing days. A policy may be that testing must be held in a controlled environment. With colleagues, a leader would then brainstorm alternative controlled sites for testing that is practical to use in the school. A procedure may be that the library must be closed during testing hours. So a leader would next focus brainstorming on the times the library *is* open during the testing day and whether those time periods be effectively used for circulation.

A leader would also consider suggested alternatives such as putting books on a cart and taking them to classes or study halls. The people affected by a closed library are students and staff. The leader would ask the group to brainstorm how to minimize the impact on students and staff. Perhaps the solution is to institute a library reserve system that allows students to reserve books that the librarian delivers to students' classrooms. The machinery impacted involves using library computers for testing. Are there any other ways to bring computers into the building or to move a number of computers to another location?

In problem solving, leaders use groups to brainstorm solutions for each cause impacting the effect. Mapping each cause and effect, in a tool such as a fishbone diagram, visually shows the relationship between the problem and the perceived causes. Once causes have been identified then brainstorming solutions is possible. The librarian in a school with this problem used a fishbone diagram; the process resulted in the creation of a master calendar on which all testing dates and locations were identified. According to the new schedule, testing was moved to areas where it made minimal impact on programs. For example, the cafeteria was designated as a location for some of the testing that took place early in the morning and later in the afternoon.

When leaders problem solve using cause and effect to form decisions, they explore a variety of issues and solutions. "Making decisions and picking the courses of action are the most critical aspects of being in charge because it is risky and very difficult" (Safi and Burrell 2007, 2). Using problem solving skills with well-developed tools such as a fishbone diagram creates an unemotional and rational method to decide on a course of action. When colleagues are involved in brainstorming effective solutions to problems then they are more likely to be supportive of the decisions and outcomes.

## THE BUCK STOPS HERE

Leaders and librarians accept responsibility for making decisions. The format or style of decision making is secondary to use of critical thinking and problem solving skills to reach conclusions that benefit the organization and its users. Although making no decision *is* a decision, effective leaders know that stagnation is the outcome of maintaining the status quo. If problems arise then decisions must be made. Thoughtful gathering of information and data assists leaders in making tough decisions. Shared or group decision making develops leadership qualities in colleagues. As President Truman knew, however, leaders are responsible for making, implementing and being accountable for decisions. Decision making is the job of leaders.

## LEADERSHIP TIPS RELATED TO DECISION MAKING

▶ Recognize that decision making comes in many styles and each carries specific responsibilities for leaders.

▶ Remember that shared decision making requires high-level involvement  and high performance from colleagues in the organization.

▶ Apply critical-thinking skills and problem-solving skills to every decision from the smallest to the largest.

▶ Demonstrate critical thinking by sifting through the confusion to find important data.

▶ Recognize that not making a decision often causes bad decisions to occur downstream.

▶ Move beyond worry of negative results and base sound decisions on critical-thinking strategies to be a responsible leader and to move the organization toward its goals.

▶ Use well-constructed tools to take the emotion out of solving problems and provide a process for solving future problems.

▶ Relinquish control in shared decision making.

▶ Create an environment of inclusiveness by using the format of shared decision making.

▶ Remember that leaders are responsible for making, implementing, and being accountable for decisions.

# Chapter 16

# Recognizing Contributions

**Leadership questions related to recognizing the contributions of others are:**

▶ Are extrinsic or intrinsic awards more motivating?

▶ Do rewards matter?

▶ What are the pitfalls to recognition?

Leaders are responsible for adding value and making a sustainable difference to the operations of an organization. Providing recognition to colleagues is one method of adding value and supporting sustainability. Every employee receives baseline rewards such as "salary, contract payments, some benefits, and a few perks" (Pink 2009, 35). Baseline reward should be sufficient for a job well done. Actually, the job well done is the reward. Navy SEAL Brandon Webb wants to know that colleagues excel in what they do. He has written that excellence is due to "pure commitment, honed over time into the fabric of excellence" (2012, 380). In a Navy SEAL's job, the reward for commitment and excellence is saving lives. In life-and-death situations the honor of a job well done, saving lives, is the highest validation for performance. Brandon Webb remarked,

"Whatever it is that you do, you are making a stand, either for excellence or mediocrity" (Webb 2012, 380).

Every leader understands that mediocre work is unacceptable. The truth is that leaders expect exemplary efforts. Colleagues who are average performers need to be encouraged to contribute their part, no matter how small it may seem, to the goals of the organization. So what motivates people to perform above and beyond the baseline of their job when completion of routine tasks should be enough of a reward? The responsibility of leaders is to cultivate an environment that demonstrates a commitment toward excellence by embedding recognition for a job well done into the culture of the organization.

Rewards are motivational and fall into two different categories, extrinsic and intrinsic. In his book *Drive*, Daniel Pink writes extensively about the impact extrinsic and intrinsic rewards have in influencing workers. He states that most organizations configure motivational programs around the assumption that "the way to improve performance, increase productivity, and encourage excellence is to reward the good and punish the bad" (2009, 19). Accountability measures provide targets to indicate that a job is done well. The reality of targets is that they prove the job was completed but do not measure efficiency or effectiveness of the work.

## EXTRINSIC VS. INTRINSIC REWARDS

Many educators realize that all too often testing in schools shows what information is remembered but does not measure understanding of underlying concepts. An example is when students were asked to choose one of four answers in a multiple-choice question designed to identify stems and leaves. Students appeared to master the concept by identifying the correct answer. In fact, they were able to find the right answer because only one answer out of the four choices had the same numbers as those in the question. Later students were given the same question, but instead of selecting a multiple-choice answer, they were required to select the stems and the leaves and place each in a graph with two columns, one for stems and the second column for leaves. Teachers found that students could not do this higher-level task because they never understood the concept in the first place.

Students taking multiple-choice tests are frequently able to figure out the right answer by eliminating choices. They receive an extrinsic reward of a passing grade, but, as these students progress to more complex math problems that are based on stems and leaves, they have difficulty. In the more challenging test students who answered the question correctly were intrinsically rewarded because they understood a concept that would assist them in more difficult problems.

One of the drawbacks of extrinsic reward as evidenced in the math example is that setting the target for success too low encourages negative or average long-term results. Students' benefited intrinsically by raising the complexity of the math task. Rewards are meaningful when extrinsic recognitions are based on performance where challenges lead to intrinsic motivation.

## WINNING COMBINATION: INTRINSIC REWARDS PLUS VALIDATION THROUGH RECOGNITION

People getting intrinsic rewards still need validation through recognition. Ralph Waldo Emerson wrote that "the reward of a thing well done is having done it" (Emerson 2013). A leader who motivates through intrinsic rewards encourages colleagues to systematically take on increasingly complex and challenging tasks. The satisfaction derived from completing these jobs is the internal or intrinsic reward. Intrinsic rewards feed a desire to accept more challenging tasks because colleagues are motivated to figure out and work on tasks that are increasingly difficult. The theories related to intrinsic motivation range from Maslow's (1943) self-actualization to McGregor's (1960) Theory Y and McClelland's (1961) achievement motivation theory that indicate mastering difficult tasks is driven by internal desires. As theories expanded over time, the common theme related to intrinsic motivation revolved around colleagues' need to successfully perform a challenging task (Wiersma 1992).

School librarians understand the power of intrinsic rewards. The library is a place where intrinsic rewards are the outcome when students find an answer to a question, research a topic and solve a problem, or create knowledge by reworking evidence. The inner satisfaction that results from expending energy to solve a need is the reward. In students, personal success is evident through completion of a project after research, and in colleagues, inner satisfaction is finishing a project to accomplish an assigned goal.

Daniel Pink explains that internal motivation is cultivated by the environment that leaders build. The environments that make people feel good about participating, while giving them freedom to go at their own pace, encourages intrinsic motivation. Leaders also stimulate intrinsic motivation by attaching a need to a cause greater than themselves (2009, 133). Mastering an assigned task that is bigger than they have ever tried before pushes the limits of colleagues' knowledge and scope of experience. Leaders who provide for experimentation and risk taking create an environment where colleagues drive themselves toward excellence. Even these self-motivating tasks are important to recognize.

Sincere recognition is critical to effective rewards. Leaders who provide genuine comments based on thoughtful reflection of the work accomplished are appreciated. Showing evidence that they know the person and his or her quality of work validates the recognition. Robert K. Cooper has suggested that leaders who talk about obstacles encountered and how individuals dealt with pressures surrounding completion of the job provide a heartfelt tone to recognitions (2001). Effective recognition is accomplished by acknowledging the individual's unique contribution toward a measured goal rather than generalized remarks that come across as superficial and meaningless.

If groups are being recognized, leaders need to interject specific comments about each of the contributors' efforts toward reaching the goal. Complimenting people on the final results and the impact those results have on the organization show recipients that the leader understands the relationship between the efforts of colleagues and the success of the organization. Personal acknowledgement that targets specific measurable results is an example of effective, informed recognition.

One way to provide effective recognition is to connect rewards and recognition to the culture of the organization. Using the organizations' heroes as metaphors for awards validates the receiver of the award by connecting individual actions with a larger-than-life model. This connection reaffirms and reminds colleagues of the basic principles upon which the organization was formed. Effective recognition will "call on the past, relate it to the present, and then use them both to provide a link to the future" (Phillips 1991, 169).

For example, a leader in a school named after Abraham Lincoln might call on the past by stating that when Mr. Lincoln was elected president of the United States he was faced with challenges that required exceptional resolve and courage. The leader could relate these challenges to the present by saying, "This year our school was engaged in a battle to raise student achievement to levels never before accomplished." Then, building on the past and present, the leader acknowledges the future by stating, "The vision President Lincoln had for our country—to resolve problems and free all citizens—is like the determination you used to overcome the obstacles preventing our students from succeeding. Our students' individual successes are a result of the hours you spent understanding your students and planning how to engage them in meaningful work. By internalizing concepts in relevant tasks they reaped successful results that brought our school to a level of excellence never before achieved." Connecting comments to the heroes and culture of the organization instills pride in individual accomplishments as well as group successes. Using this format when recognizing colleagues, validates and motivates team members.

## VALUE OF SIGNIFICANT EXTRINSIC REWARDS

Extrinsic rewards do have their place, especially in validating excellence in a profession and in serving as advocacy tools. In this case, awards and public recognitions are the responsibility of leaders of professional organizations. AASL sponsors awards to identify individuals and groups that show evidence of sustained efforts to build effective school library programs. AASL awards encourage support for exemplary practices and successful implementation of standards outlined in *Empowering Learners* and *Standards for the 21st-Century Learner*. Some awards include monetary contributions to the further success of the program, some awards are in the form of grants, and some awards bestow prestigious trophies.

The real importance in these awards and grants is confirmation that best practices are producing great school library programs, that corporations support school librarians, and that individuals value school libraries. The awards and grants are advocacy tools that symbolize how school libraries and librarians are contributing to student achievement. At the same time, these awards and grants recognize members' efforts to promote excellence.

## POSITIVE OUTCOMES

Leaders know that recognition of a job done well provides a spike in performance. More importantly this recognition promotes an environment where colleagues are committed to risk taking and excellence. Whether using a personal handwritten note, an e-mail message that is also sent to colleagues and administrator, or a face-to-face acknowledgement, successful leaders recognize the efforts of colleagues. Leaders understand the benefits of developing an environment where intrinsic rewards motivate employees toward a committed quest for excellence.

When I was a high school librarian I wrote notes to parents each day letting them know their child was exemplary in the library. Sometimes I would highlight an act of kindness, such as helping another student, or provide a brief description of the initiative the student exhibited when researching, or supply evidence that the student showed mastery of an inquiry process. Parents loved these little notes. The student received an intrinsic reward by accomplishing something extraordinary. The note provided additional recognition. The notes also help the library program achieve its goals; students whose efforts had been recognized were enthusiastic about continuing to strive for excellence.

Leaders also know that extrinsic rewards are meaningful as well. Framed certificates, formal recognition at a school board meeting, gift cards from local businesses, flowers, or a coupon to leave work a few hours early let colleagues know that their leaders are grateful for a job done well. The organization benefits from the continued efforts of workers who have received positive reinforcement for their good work.

When students displayed work in the library, such as a work of art or the results of a research project, I would take a picture of the display and e-mail it to the parents. On the high school level I gave out coupons for five dollars from the local gas station. Students loved those rewards and came into the library to participate in contests such as the question of the day or the SAT word of the day. They had fun, and I reinforced the idea that the library was a good place to be.

Daniel Pink encourages leaders "to set aside an entire day where employees can work on anything they choose, however they want, with whomever they'd like." One outcome of this day is that people must bring in a new idea, resource, or process to work the next day (2009, 169). This type of reward encourages innovation, camaraderie, and fun. It rewards colleagues by providing them with an opportunity to solve challenges in an open and unrestrained atmosphere. Leaders know that truly committed workers are compelled by a culture of excellence. That excellence needs to be recognized by authentic praise as well as by intrinsic satisfaction.

## LEADERSHIP TIPS RELATED TO RECOGNIZING THE EFFORTS OF OTHERS

▶ Remember that leaders are responsible for adding value and making a sustainable difference to the operations of an organization.

▶ Provide recognitions that energize and motivate colleagues toward a higher level of performance and excellence.

▶ Validate intrinsic rewards through recognition.

▶ Recognize that intrinsic motivation is the inner satisfaction that results from expending energy to solve a need.

▶ Motivate through intrinsic rewards to encourage colleagues to systematically take on increasingly complex and challenging tasks.

▶ Provide genuine comments based on thoughtful reflection of the work accomplished; such comments are appreciated because they show evidence of the leader knowing the person.

▶ Provide effective recognition by acknowledging the individual's unique contribution toward a measured goal.

▶ Avoid general remarks that come across as superficial and meaningless.

▶ Use the organization's heroes as metaphors for awards; such statements validate, reaffirm, and remind colleagues of the basic principles upon which the organization was formed.

▶ Recognize that awards and recognitions are the responsibility of leaders of professional organizations to validate excellence in the profession.

▶ Stimulate a spike in performance by providing recognition of a job done well.

▶ Provide colleagues with an opportunity to solve challenges in an open and unrestrained atmosphere; this opportunity serves as a motivational reward and benefits the organization through innovative thinking.

# Section 5
## Truth North

In *Lincoln*, the 2012 movie from Steven Spielberg, Lincoln is explaining his strategy for passage of the 13th amendment to Thaddeus Stevens, the powerful House Ways and Means chair. Stevens, a staunch abolitionist, is concerned about Lincoln's evasiveness on the issue of slavery, and "urges unwavering adherence to a moral compass that points unambiguously toward 'True North'" (Snyder 2012). With caring and deliberate speech, Lincoln sympathetically reminds Stevens that while a compass needle shows you where true north is, it doesn't tell you what is between you and the end point. He explains that sometimes you can get stuck in a swamp if you take the direct route, and you may never reach your goal. In this case, getting the amendment passed was more important than losing the entire vote due to following a more direct route that included uncompromising views.

Leaders know the most effective journey is often winding and circuitous, and if you can't make that journey to completion, what good is it to know where true north is? Leaders assess and evaluate processes, people, and forward momentum. Without self-assessment, deep reflection, and evidence-based practices road blocks are raised, and leadership fails to be innovative and set inspiration for future direction.

# Chapter 17

# Reflection

**Leadership questions related to reflection are:**

▶ How does personal self-reflection contribute to leadership?

▶ What are process checks?

▶ Are there tools that assist in assessing processes?

Four students sat at the table on the left; four sat at the table on the right; a moderator stood between them. Book Bowl, a battle-of-the-books-type competition, was in full swing, and these students were competing for bragging rights as the champion book bowl team. Hundreds of fifth-grade students from thirty-two schools spent the previous summer reading, discussing, and studying the themes, plots, settings, and characters in thirty books. To an observer it was an example of teamwork as each question in round one was voiced, and members conferred before deciding on the final answer. Successful book bowl students know they must work together in preliminary rounds, creating confidence as the team chooses thoughtful answers. In the final round, students buzz in to individually answer questions.

The key to winning book bowl is to ensure that each answer in the first couple of rounds is correct. Conferring enables members to reflect and compare individual answers and then decide on the best response. In the final round students rely on their own abilities to analyze the information and decide on the needed answer. Impulsiveness has no place in this competition that depends on accuracy. Mental concentration and careful consideration is the definition of reflection as well as of the book bowl teams' thought process (Farlex 2012a). Without reflective studying, the teams fail. Through reflection team members learn how to self-assess their content knowledge in the books. In self-assessing their knowledge students find out what they know and what they do not know.

## SELF-REFLECTION FOR LEADERS

Self-reflection is where leadership matures. Leaders who reflect on their style of leadership examine their own thinking, motives, actions, and habits. Self-assessment is a learning experience through which patterns emerge. Some of these patterns show successful results while others indicate unproductive or ineffective outcomes. Generally, people repeat the same thinking and actions. Through self-reflection habits that need changing are identified. Effective leaders become conscious of those unproductive actions and work to develop and use more effective thinking to accomplish tasks. Leaders who incorporate reflective inquiry into their personal leadership habits facilitate self-understanding. The result of this understanding is an assessment of how and why their actions or inactions bring forth recurring results.

One of the realities I learned early on in my career is that administrators like to help, but often do not have solutions readily available. Every day administrators deal with problem after problem involving students, teachers, support staff, and the community. When I was in my twenties I volunteered to work on the neighborhood swimming pool committee. The chair of the committee told all of us that if we had a problem with the way something was being done then we needed to bring a solution with the concern. His premise was that he did not want to spend time working on unresolvable problems. This tactic made all of us on the committee think through our suggestions. It saved the committee time because proposals were often positive with effective resolutions.

When I coach school librarians under my supervision I explain that every problem will be solved faster and supported by administration if you, the librarian, bring possible solutions to the administrator when problems arise. I spend a good deal of time brainstorming the causes of issues with librarians, and then together we identify possible solutions. A result of our conversation is reflection about the issues and actions impacting the problems. We review all stakeholders' needs, fears, and wants. When the librarian does meet with administration about a problem and brings possible solutions of ways administration can help, then the chance of support is high.

Reflective librarians display initiative and understanding of the issues contributing to a problem. This is leadership because they are taking ownership of a problem and developing suggestions to create successful resolution. Each reflective glance at thoughts, actions, habits, and motives of others creates a learning experience that deepens effective leadership style. Leaders can learn how to be more effective by reflecting on their own responses to the actions of others. Were their own responses counterproductive? Could a similar situation be handled more effectively in the future? How?

In Jim Collins's book *Good to Great* he explained leadership qualities that transform companies into accomplished organizations. The premise of his book (2001, 5) is whether a good company can become great and if so how? The answer is leadership that he describes as level 5 leadership. He compares level 5 leaders to Abraham Lincoln and Socrates, whom he characterize as "a study in duality: modest and willful, humble and fearless" (2001, 22). Collins looked to leaders who set up an infrastructure that lasted long after the leader was gone.

As Collins studied level 5 leadership he found several interesting qualities. One such quality is what he termed the "window and the mirror." Leaders who are great look out the window and give credit to factors outside themselves when things go well. At the same time, these leaders look in the mirror when assigning responsibility, never blaming others when things go bad (2001, 35). This mirror image—reflective assessment of each decision and action—makes a difference in leaders who are great.

## APPLYING SKILLS LIBRARIANS ALREADY HAVE

School librarians have the ability to be effective self-assessors of their leadership style. The "window and mirror" method of reflection is a quality librarians use when they work with students and staff, encouraging them when they do well and reflecting back over library practices to improve user experiences. School librarians encourage students to reflect on the results of information seeking, synthesis, and application of knowledge. Librarians do this because self-assessment is integral to AASL's *Standards for the 21st-Century Learner*. Reflection and self-assessment is a strand in each of the four learning standards (AASL 2007).

After years of observing librarians who incorporate student self-assessment into lessons, I now observe that students use higher-level thinking when researching and solving inquiry problems. In addition, the students' process of metacognition or knowledge about their thinking intrinsically changes student habits. Students know why they are selecting specific resources and how they reached conclusions. Students are making good decisions about their learning while forming reflective habits that will help them be successful in the future. Reflection deepens student understanding and enables changes to be made based on evidence they compiled while assessing their work. This learning experience can be replicated by librarians to deepen their own understanding of their leadership practices.

Leaders embrace reflective thinking to assess what they know and what they do not know, what processes in place are successful, and what practices need to be changed. Albert Einstein explained that, "The significant problems we face today cannot be solved at the same level of thinking with which we created them" (Einstein 2009). Successful leaders recognize that the principle behind self-awareness is to encourage higher-level thinking and productive problem solving. Reflection opens new avenues for decision making that impacts meaningful change.

## REAL-LIFE EXAMPLE

Many leadership situations involve assessing problems to deliver a viable solution. When I was working on my Master's degree, the Total Quality Management philosophy based on the work of W. Edwards Deming was being used in many businesses. From studying the work of Deming I learned to look at the processes behind the results to be more effective and efficient in the future. Leaders take outcomes, review resulting data, and evaluate any points of failure in order to make future improvements (Schmoker 1994). With Total Quality Management, improvement is the goal, and leaders incorporate process checks into their work. This means that when an activity is undertaken, periodic checks are made as the project progresses. No event or activity that involves multiple steps should flow forward without regular stops to ensure targets are being met.

One of the most complex tasks I was assigned was to develop a method through which school librarians' instruction could be tied to individual student achievement. In the past, data was collected to confirm that groups of students performed well academically when they frequented the library but having to verify that a librarian improved achievement for a specific student was daunting. My district gave me an end date for the project. I began by discussing the concept with my counterparts in other curriculum areas before deciding on a method. Then I developed rubrics where the student targets for achievement were the indicators in AASL's *Standards for the 21st-Century Learner.*

At this point I could have finalized the processes and grading guide, and presented them to the librarians to implement. Instead I sent all eight-two school librarians the draft for review. Once I had received comments, I revised the instruments. Once again I could have considered that the project was done. Instead, I took a new revision before a committee composed of six school librarians: two elementary school, two middle school, and two high school. This committee met once a month over four months, revising the language in the document and adjusting the process tools because the practical application of the documents revealed a need for adjustments. At each meeting the tools were refined until a workable process evolved.

The final product was presented to the librarians in the district for comments a month before the product was due. Once the district leadership approved the process, I worked with the committee to develop a training module as a means of introducing the final process to the librarians in the district. One of the goals for the training was to provide real-life examples and best practices for using the assessment tools. Although the new process was a major instructional change, it was met with acceptance due to the many process checks and refinements throughout the developmental phase.

## BENEFITS OF REFLECTION

Every school librarian has a major event, curriculum idea, or program change to implement. With large, complex assignments librarians who are leaders periodically test the ideas and plans for accuracy and feasibility. This reflection by leaders with input from stakeholders creates success. Leaders who are open to letting others comment and examine new ideas discover that this input and reflection help identify problems to be fixed and misunderstandings that can be clarified.

When I was a high school librarian I always asked a student to test my instructions on how to access and use a particular database. My goal was to make sure that the process was succinct and clear. If the steps were too involved, students would lose interest and abandon the database for something quicker. The student assessment in this case made the process and instructions effective and assured success. Incorporating reflection ensures new endeavors are workable. This reflection may change a leader's thinking about what is needed to meet goals and achieve success. As Albert Einstein stated, thinking must change in order to solve today's problems.

"Reflective tools can help leaders take stock of their situations and imagine new possibilities for action" (Knapp, Copland, and Talbert 2003, 6). The data and information collected using reflective processes assists leaders in confirming what they consider important while allowing them to understand where misperceptions and misunderstandings exist. Leaders implement reflective techniques to gain perspective of what influences decisions and reactions among those they serve.

Reflection is achieved in different ways. A leader may journal daily successes and disappointments to gain insight into what thinking, actions, and habits worked well and which did not. Creating panels of stakeholders to reflect on policies and procedures is an effective means for gaining feedback. These stakeholders can comment publicly or privately in writing or face-to-face. Seeking stakeholder input is important because a leader receives input about the idea from those who are primarily impacted by the plan. Committees of experts serve as a means of reflection as each contributes unique ideas and discusses possibilities before morphing key principles into worthwhile concepts. Shared leadership is reflective and provides inspiration for moving the organization forward. Leaders create unity in the organization every time they use reflection by including members of the organization in decision making and developing strategic goals.

An additional benefit is that leaders begin to emerge from within the organization as individuals are involved in developing policies, making decisions, and creating processes. According to Jim Collins in his book *Good to Great*, a leader sets up an infrastructure that lasts long after the leader is gone. Leaving a legacy of success is accomplished through building an inclusive organization where input is welcomed and valued. Leaders who model reflective practices encourage individuals within the organization to incorporate reflective practices into their own task evaluation. When technological and ideological demands arise, members of the organization make instrumental changes based on reflective input as new methods develop. Leaders who use reflective practices embed them into the culture of the organization. Leadership throughout the organization matures and the legacy of excellence continues.

## LEADERSHIP TIPS RELATED TO REFLECTION

▶ Remember that mental concentration and careful consideration is the definition of reflection.

▶ Recognize that leadership matures through personal self-reflection.

▶ Reflect on your style of leadership by examining your own thinking, motives, actions, and habits.

▶ Use self-reflection to identify habits that need changing.

▶ Understand how and why your own actions or inactions as leader bring forth recurring results.

▶ Embrace reflective thinking to assess what you know and what you do not know, what processes in place are successful, and what practices need to be changed.

▶ Inspect the outcomes, review the resulting data, and evaluate any points of failure in order to make future improvements.

▶ Stop periodically during events and activities that involve multiple steps to ensure targets are being met.

▶ Model reflective practices to encourage individuals within the organization to incorporate reflective practices into their task evaluation.

▶ Implement reflective techniques to gain perspective of what influences decisions and reactions among those served.

# Chapter 18

# Innovation

**Leadership questions related to innovation are:**

▶ Why does maintaining the status quo prove unacceptable to innovative leaders?

▶ What key attributes encourage innovation?

▶ How do leaders nurture a culture of innovation?

If the name Henriette Davidson Avram has no meaning to you, it should. She was called "a pioneer of the information age at the Library of Congress" by James H. Billington, Librarian of Congress (Schudel 2006). She used her talents as a computer programmer and systems analyst to develop what librarians call MARC (Machine Readable Cataloging) format. A 1989 article in *American Libraries* magazine said she "launched a revolution in libraries" and was "one of the century's most influential library leaders." (Schudel 2006). Her work standardizing a digital format for library records in 1968 changed the library catalog and provided a means for electronic catalogs, facilitated interlibrary loans, and more-efficient processing of library materials. MARC format was adopted nationally and internationally as the standard cataloging protocol. Her innovative work helped transform libraries from warehouses of print materials and artifacts to automated information hubs for communities. During the emerging computer age her work set the direction of library services for generations.

Although Henriette Avram was not a librarian when "she was charged with devising a way to compile and disseminate bibliographic records by computer," she worked with catalogers to innovate library access. "She designed a mathematical code, using cataloging numbers, letters and symbols to denote different elements, or fields, of bibliographic information" (Schudel 2006). The result changed the status quo for libraries.

Describing innovation must include a description of the status quo because they are two opposite ends of a continuum. Too often leaders are afraid to change the status quo, defined as the existing state of operations (Farlex 2012b). Running an organization the way it has always been ran is easier than making changes. The problem with keeping things the same is that the world will pass you by. Every profession must be innovative and embrace change or become irrelevant.

In education three factors discourage innovation and encourage the status quo. They are fear of failure, fear of fallout, and fear of change (Hawkins 2012). The fear of failure comes from the notion that past mistakes will continue even if changes are made. This was evident when people in Montgomery County, Maryland, decided to open a charter school. The education leaders did not believe that a change like this would improve academic results for the targeted students. Fear of political fallout resulted when the administrators became concerned that scores would drop on specific tests. In the Maryland example, part of the plan for the charter school was to allow targeted underperforming students to take the SAT test. Principals and other educational leaders feared that parents would become vocal and concerned if the overall average SAT score for the county decreased. The third factor encouraging leaders to maintain the status quo in education is fear of change. In the Maryland charter school example, certain populations were considered privileged and elite programs were offered only to wealthier communities. When the charter school decided to implement an International Baccalaureate (IB) program, the educational leaders feared a negative outcry from parents resistant to change (Hawkins 2012).

## CALCULATED RISKS

Successful leaders understand that allowing the status quo to continue is more frightening than the risk of innovation. Leaders encourage innovation so that the future of the organization remains relevant. Currently discussion is taking place in the library profession about how to best incorporate technology, social networking, and e-books into school libraries. Conversations are good; action is better. The insight of the Librarian of Congress in 1968 when Henriette Avram was asked to create a link between library records and digital technology created sustainability for library programs. School librarians who are innovative understand the direct relationship between innovation and staying relevant.

Leaders who encourage innovation are calculated risk takers. They minimize risk by segmenting a project and researching each part. Smart risk takers explore new ideas and document what worked and what did not. After a thorough analysis of any idea, leaders make improvements and move forward. The resulting data is important in reducing risk. The more adept innovative leaders are at addressing calculated risk, the better those leaders are at developing processes that create success.

A risk-analysis process that works for me is to create a plan for a specific change, implement that change, check what was successful, and then revise the plan. Introducing e-books into the district proved to be challenging due to publisher restrictions on use by school libraries. Over several years I continued to collect data and urged vendors to find answers to questions impacting implementation of an e-book solution. Some of the questions considered prior to implementation included: Would the district would own the e-books or rent them and be charged a yearly fee? Would apps be available for the myriad of student- owned devices? What would network requirements be? Were bibliographic records available for the titles? Compiling the questions and then waiting for vendor solutions took time.

The e-book launch was successful for the school librarians because student users and risks were reevaluated each time a set of questions were answered. Risk is minimized when leaders document what is effective through each step of the process. Any new endeavor contains risks. Leaders reduce that risk by asking questions, researching answers, and revising the project based on evaluation of known results.

## OPENNESS

Looking beyond obvious solutions is the attribute of an innovative leader. When ideas arise, whether they are improvements to existing programs, policies, and projects or completing new initiatives, the first barrage of solutions are predictable rather than unique. Effective leaders permit wait-time when colleagues brainstorm a variety of ideas. To allow deeper thinking and outside-the-box ideas to surface, leaders patiently wait when requesting teams to solve a problem. Innovative leaders intentionally encourage suggestions for multiple solutions from team members. These ideas align team members' thoughts and reinforce the idea that all contribute to solving problems.

When leaders use teams to explore innovative ideas a variety of experiences and levels of expertise is brought to problem solving. Those in leadership positions accept or reject team solutions. Sometimes problems arise, and leaders need to make more-spontaneous decisions without the benefit of team consensus. However, just as wait-time benefits the generation of solutions for teams, leaders use wait-time to marshal their own thoughts. Pausing to assess all solutions related to a decision invites more creative team and individual ideas.

## CULTURE OF INNOVATION

A culture of innovation is encouraged by leaders who clearly identify innovation as an important focus of the organization and ensure that organizational structure will not hinder colleagues' creativity. They encourage colleagues' innovation through stories and recounting past successes. In addition, leaders who value innovation establish organizational parameters that allow colleagues to feel free to work on creative problem solving.

Google is a company often noted for its culture of innovation. "It is reputed to have its employees spend 60% of their time on the job, 30% being helpful to others, and 10% thinking" (BlessingWhite 2007, 4). Knowing that time is built into the day to be creative and to think is important, but mandating creativity does not always result in innovation. Creative thinking results when colleagues know leaders trust and support their ideas. Leaders who are active listeners and create multiple avenues for colleagues to contribute ideas inspire members in the organization to offer ideas. In a culture of innovation each suggestion that surfaces is accepted and reviewed for further study. Once an idea is implemented, leaders understand the importance of supporting results to encourage additional innovative ideas. Consequently, an essential leadership skill is supporting colleagues when solutions are unsuccessful because leaders turn failures into lessons learned (BlessingWhite 2007, 11). Through this acceptance innovative leaders promote a sense of freedom that leads to a culture of innovation.

Apple is a company that prides itself on innovation. The company's management appreciates those who see things differently and push the boundaries. Decision makers at Apple respect creative minds when they approve a commercial that says, in part, "And while some may see them as the crazy ones, we see genius. Because the people who are crazy enough to think they can change the world, are the ones who do" (Goodreads 2013).

## FOSTERING INNOVATION

Developing practices that encourage innovation is the sign of a forward-thinking leader. In Daniel Pink's book *Drive*, he explains that the secret to motivation is "our deep seated desire to direct our own lives, to extend and expand our abilities, and to live a life of purpose" (2009, 145). Great leaders motivate those they work with by empowering them to make job related decisions that extend their knowledge and skills in meaningful ways. Leaders who are visionary identify talented people who reflect on new ideas and, ultimately, change the organization. Innovative leadership means providing opportunities for colleagues to collaborate and solve problems that surface due to new technologies.

Suzanne Fetscher has stated that leaders hold the key to transforming traditional organizations into innovative cultures. In her article "Innovative Cultures," she mentions six ways that leaders can stimulate innovation. These include giving colleagues time and encouragement to connect with their creativity to solve business problems without micro-management from the boss. In addition, she stated that colleagues need a place to be creative. Leaders can stimulate creativity by bringing in outside experts who energize workers and inspire creativity (Fetscher 2008). Leaders who develop a culture of innovation need to be willing to stand behind new ideas and methods and to encourage acceptance of new concepts.

## APPLYING SKILLS LIBRARIANS ALREADY HAVE

School librarians model best practice when encouraging innovation in students. They know that students thrive when they direct their own learning because they are intrinsically rewarded as their skills and knowledge base is extended. Students work more effectively when research projects are problem-based, relevant, and meaningful. Students who are given open access to the library are provided with the time and space to be creative with the results of their research. The librarian who works collaboratively with teachers to stimulate creative thinking based on data and research is encouraging engaging learning and innovation.

The same principles create leadership opportunities for librarians when faced with making innovative changes to the library program. School librarians are innovative; they are visionary and are anything but the stereotypical view of the librarian behind the desk who quiets the customers. School libraries are active laboratories were information access and flexible physical space combine to encourage relevant learning. School librarians brought innovation into the schools through the online catalog and computer management program. In many school districts libraries were the first place in the schools to use computers to streamline tedious repetitive work in a meaningful way. Later the introduction of databases that changed from CD technology to web-based access was first brought to schools through librarians.

Using blogs for online interactive curriculum and book discussions, social networking to deliver information to students, and web-based video sites to deliver student research products are all examples of ways school librarians are continuing to push the boundaries and maintain relevance for staff and students. In addition, by fully implementing AASL's *Standards for the 21st Century Learner* and *Empowering Learners: Guidelines for School Library Programs* school librarians are setting the lead for curriculum delivery in ways that help students learn how to develop skills and dispositions that enable them to be responsible self-assessors of their work. The learning standards change the focus from assessing specific learning targets to learning how to assess how effectively work is accomplished.

In the assessment-driven drill and kill learning environment, librarians are stimulating engaging teaching strategies among colleagues. This is innovation at its best. Teachers who collaborate with librarians learn how to implement innovative instructional strategies that motivate student learning and stimulate inquiry. Recently a sixth grade science teacher came to a librarian in my district seeking help with a unit on fossil fuels. Through a teaching consultation the librarian guided the teacher from a typical report on fossil fuels into an engaging innovative lesson. The librarian suggested that the teacher have students create an essential question about fossil fuels as it related to a real life problem. She explained that in order to answer this question the students would need to research the topic and demonstrate how their new knowledge impacted their perspective on the question. Students guided by their teacher decided they wanted to know if there was an alternative fuel that would power school buses and save the county money. A technology instructor teamed with the teacher and librarian on the project and assisted students as they created varied products presenting the results of their research. The students presented their results to the Director of Transportation and to their School Board Representative. In addition, the students' research and outcomes stimulated questions about why the school district was not using alternative fuels. What started as a routine lesson evolved into an active learning experience that was motivating for all. Librarians have the ability to model, guide, and motivate colleagues. When librarians collaborate with teachers they empower colleagues to make instructional changes that extend students' knowledge and skills in meaningful ways. Librarians directly foster innovation among colleagues.

## LEADERSHIP TIPS RELATED TO INNOVATION

- ▶ Recognize that status quo and innovation are two opposite ends of a continuum.
- ▶ Help colleagues get past the three factors that discourage innovation and encourage the status quo: fear of failure, fear of fallout, and fear of change.
- ▶ Avoid permitting fear to prevent innovation and allow the status quo to stand; the results of giving in to the fear are more frightening than the risks.
- ▶ Be a risk taker by encouraging innovation.
- ▶ Look beyond obvious solutions.
- ▶ Encourage innovation in small issues as well as large issues.
- ▶ Provide opportunities for colleagues to collaborate in solving problems that surface due to new technologies.
- ▶ Go beyond developing a culture of innovation; also be willing to stand behind new ideas and methods and to encourage acceptance of new concepts.
- ▶ Recognize that mandating creativity does not always result in innovation.
- ▶ Build trust, support, and guide creativity if you want to create a culture of innovation.

# Chapter 19

# Evidenced-Based Practice

**Leadership questions related to evidence-based practice:**

▶ What is evidence-based practice?

▶ When do leaders use evidence-based practices?

▶ What steps are effective in creating evidence-based leadership model?

Arthur Conan Doyle wrote stories of intrigue about Sherlock Holmes's efforts to solve crimes by scrutinizing evidence. Like the novels *And Then There Were None* and *Murder on the Orient Express* by Agatha Christie, the Sherlock Holmes stories require readers to look at facts and seek beyond obvious evidence to make a decision about how a crime was committed and by whom. By collecting a variety of data and then judging it for relevance and truth, leaders—like investigators in mystery books—reach decisions.

Evidence-Based Practice (EBP) refers to the use of research and scientific studies as the bases for determining the best practices in a profession. The Colorado Department of Education published information about Evidence-Based Practice in which they define it as "the use of practices, interventions, and treatments which have been proven, through scientifically based research, to be effective in improving outcomes for individuals when the practice is implemented with fidelity" (2011).

Librarians teach proven research models to students to improve their research outcomes. Students who arrive at the school library with questions and need to research answers find greater success when following the Big 6 research steps or similar research processes than they do when they search randomly. In a high school library in my district, the geometry teacher begins his year in the library. Students learn about deductive reasoning through reading an Agatha Christie novel. Through an interactive blog students discuss the characters and their actions. As each chapter is read and explored students pull out incidents and evidence to solve the murder. By blogging each chapter, evidence and proof of the students' growth as they think based on logic are documented for the librarian and teacher. By the time students reach the end of the novel, they arrive at a conclusion using facts gleaned from the novel (Branyon 2013). A lesson like this is concrete practice in deductive reasoning. It provides the basis for students' future success in geometry where fact, definitions, rules, or properties provide clues to solve math problems. Librarians teach deductive reasoning when introducing research models. They also use data to form library program decisions. Evidence-Based Practice is an outgrowth of their professional training and competencies.

## APPLYING EBP

When determining best practice, decisions are impacted by how information is gathered. Leaders collect data a variety of ways. They note successful practices and apply these same practices to similar situations. Professional organizations collect and disseminate information about best practices. The AASL website is jam-packed with resources for school librarians. It contains professional tools, research and statistics, publications and journals, as well as guidelines and standards. The AASL site also has portals to professional development and access to resources for instruction. School librarians who are leaders use their professional organizations to gather information about tested policies and practices. Evidence of what works is available to librarians from professional learning communities. In my district the library webpage, committee work, formal meetings, and informal meetings provide librarians with EBP to adapt and use. Knowing *where* to gather valid information and data forms the basis of best practice.

Leaders review evidence they collect. They evaluate the data's relevance, validity, and accuracy before forming a plan of action. Relevance means that data relates to a specific need. For example, if a school librarian is attempting to determine student growth in reading then various options must be evaluated to ensure validity. Circulation statistics are easy to compile, but will circulation numbers show accurate information about student growth in reading? Generally circulation statistics do not. Some students check out books and never read them; others read books that are too easy, and still others check out books to look at the illustrations and pictures. If the need is to find out how reading impacts student growth in reading, a better indicator would be tracking a specific group of high-need students by offering them an opportunity to participate in a reading discussion group.

To collect relevant data the school librarian could begin by administering a pre-test and then conduct several book discussions. Following up the discussions by administering a post-test would determine each student's reading growth since the pre-test. Based on relevant data collected about this group of students, future programs could be created to accomplish meaningful growth in reading.

Validity of data means that the information and research has been replicated and affirmed in multiple studies. Accuracy means that the methodology and resulting conclusions are free from distortion. Using a pre-test and post-test with students to determine growth in reading skills results in an accurate assessment of growth because it shows the level of student skills at the end of a time period and compares the level to each student's reading level at the start. Showing relevance, accuracy and validity must be kept in mind from the outset when data collection is planned and performed.

"Evidence-based practice recognizes multiple sources, types of evidence, and ways of gathering evidence. The use of multiple sources facilitates triangulation—an approach to data analysis that synthesizes data from multiple sources" (Todd 2008). The importance of data in EBP is directly related to the kinds of evidence collected. Isolated instances, gut feelings, documented evidence, and irrefutable evidence provide opportunities for leaders to document support for improved practices. Each of these types of evidence is important for different reasons.

An isolated observation may inspire an idea for improvement. Librarians who observe one another often observe specific strategies and use them in their own libraries to improve instruction. In my district librarians may use professional leave to observe each other. Often they observe lessons targeting a specific instructional strategy like the use of a station approach to learning. Sometimes they observe how a specific technology tool enhances a learning experience. As a result of observing their peer's use of best practice, learning improves.

Gut feelings are a valuable barometer of a successful leader. Leaders who have an instinctive idea of what the next initiative may be are able to sense the climate of the school based on information that is communicated. Following personal intuition they can be proactive in anticipating future direction of the organization. In 1996 an article about the energy industry and the need to take a proactive stance due to anticipated deregulation was published. The industry was charged with continuing cost-effective energy-efficient projects because if deregulation was put into effect any of the industry's investments would reap benefits. The article provided best-practice ideas for energy companies to implement to be prepared for deregulation. Staying flexible, creating alliances with energy management companies, and improving specifications on new designs were among suggestions in the article. The energy industry anticipated changes based on a gut feeling about conversations in the legislature (Taking a Proactive Stance 1996). Leaders listen to conversations within and outside the organization. They prepare for the future by acting on evidence and putting proactive policies and practices into place.

Another category of data is documented evidence. Collecting statistics about what is *accomplished* rather than what was *done* to complete a task is key to documented evidence. Gathering documented evidence provides a rationale for why a particular practice is effective, so leaders use this type of data to justify practices that are effective. More importantly, they use documented evidence to improve upon current practice by adapting practices for future success.

The last type of evidence, irrefutable evidence, is based on research and knowledge. In the school library profession collecting irrefutable evidence is necessary to ensure the future of library programs. School librarians who take the lead by building evidence of library program success within their own schools are practicing leadership skills. In addition, when presenting this evidence, they include national statistics and data provided by AASL. Librarians who show irrefutable evidence that school library programs lead to student academic achievement and lifelong learning are using EBP to solidify the future of their library programs.

Leaders understand that each type of evidence collected is important and essential. Using multiple data types to triangulate the facts forms a picture of an organizations' relevance. Leaders recognize that using multiple sources of evidence forms solid groundwork to identify best practices and sustainability.

EBP started in the health-care industry and moved into education when school districts' funding depended on results from student testing and assessment. Leaders needed to gather evidence and transform data into practices to provide positive and improved test score results. School district leaders learned from the health-care industry that EBP is a complex process that comprises a number of steps. Librarians from Duke University Medical Center Library and University of North Carolina at Chapel Hill Health Sciences Library produced a document that reduces the EBP process steps to six words: assess, ask, acquire, appraise, apply, self-evaluate (Schardt and Mayer 2010).

Leaders begin assessing problems that need to be solved by asking questions. Questions need to be comprehensive and relevant to the problem. These questions form the basis for researching background information about causes contributing to the problem. Leaders acquire background data to appraise practices that may be contributing to the problem. In EBP leaders critically judge the evidence for validity, impact, and applicability to the problem. After considering the research evidence and the needed outcomes, leaders apply the information and decide on a course of action. Once implemented, leaders evaluate the practice to determine its effectiveness (Salbach and Jaglal 2011).

Leaders who collect data throughout the process find that a final evaluation of the data justifies whether changes to the practice need to be made. Positive growth results for the organization when improvements to practices generate more-efficient and effective outcomes. The more leaders use EBP as a routine strategy for addressing improved outcomes, the more proficient they become in the process.

Like the authors of mystery books who write crime-scene investigations, librarians collect evidence to create practices that solve problems. Important to their investigation and research is using resources and expertise provided by professional organizations. Leaders stay informed about best practices by attending professional workshops, reading professional journals, and participating in personal learning communities.

In 2007 *School Library Journal* hosted a national Leadership Summit that focused on EBP for school librarians. The summit emphasized how librarians should use and compare data from a number of sources. Librarians were urged to use evidence to develop convincing information about school library practices' impacts on school improvement. The summit leaders advised librarians to change from the practice of accentuating what is *done* in the school library to emphasizing what is *achieved* as a result of the library program. Librarians were given methods that changed the way data should be presented to decision makers (Todd 2008).

## APPLYING SKILLS LIBRARIANS ALREADY HAVE

AASL's *Standards for the 21st-Century Learner* stress developing students who are assessors of their work and the outcomes they create. "The standards clearly provide a framework for the evidence that should be generated. They provide a structure for making evidence-based claims about the school library's contribution to learning, and give focus to specific evidence-collecting strategies" (Todd 2008).

School librarians are charged with developing students who analyze information, draw conclusions and are self-assessors of their work. Leaders who use EBP access, analyze, apply, and evaluate information in order to improve their organization. School librarians use these very same skills when working with students. To better their school library programs, librarians must transfer their knowledge and expertise of gathering evidence and use the resulting data to ensure that the library program's relevance is understood by decision makers.

## LEADERSHIP TIPS RELATED TO EVIDENCE-BASED PRACTICE

▶ Collect a variety of evidence, and then evaluate it for relevance and truth when making decisions about practices.

▶ Be aware that decisions and results are impacted by how information is gathered, what criteria are viewed, and the kinds of evidence collected.

▶ Make a conscious note of practices that are successful and apply them to similar situations.

▶ Know where to gather information and understand the validity of the data found; these skills form the basis of establishing what is best practice.

▶ Remember that relevance means that data impacts a specific need.

▶ Use valid data, which is based on research that has been replicated and affirmed in multiple studies.

▶ Recognize that accuracy depends on the methodology and resulting conclusions being free from distortion.

▶ Collect data while keeping in mind that the data must be shown to be relevant, accurate, and valid.

▶ Remember that an isolated observation may inspire an idea for improvement.

▶ Document what is accomplished rather than what was done; such evidence will be powerful support for the school library program.

# Chapter 20

## Understanding the Future

**Leadership questions related to understanding the future are:**

▶ Did Thomas Jefferson provide a roadmap for understanding the future?

▶ What are essential qualities a leader needs to understand the future?

▶ How can school librarians prepare for the future?

Because of the rapid pace of changes in our society and our technology, envisioning how to manage the future of our library programs seems difficult. However, the future becomes clear when we reflect on the past and move forward. When implementing change, how do leaders cope with the fact that the future is today, immediate, and constantly shifting? Leaders understand that every moment is the most important moment because waiting until tomorrow to change is too late. They use what they know today to benefit the future of library users and library programs.

Leaders provide insight on how to move forward by reflecting and analyzing the past. The resulting insights enable leaders to be change agents in their organizations. For library programs to survive librarians must be visionary leaders who combine time-tested values of the profession with a passion for innovation. When I was president of Virginia's state school library professional organization I instituted the Future Trends and Issues Committee. The goal of this committee was to give members a glimpse into what was coming down the road. Information about the future is relevant to current change, and leaders must use gathered information to make adjustments and maneuver new approaches, technologies, and practices while bringing about relevant library program reform.

## LESSONS FROM A FOUNDING FATHER

Many forward-thinking leaders are readers. One example from the early days of our country is Thomas Jefferson, who was a voracious reader and created a library of books on various topics from philosophy to farming. Thomas Jefferson chose the words "memory," "reason," and "imagination" as the basis for organizing knowledge in his library because he felt those words best described the material contained in each section. History books were filed under memory, philosophy books under reason, and fine arts information under imagination.

When Thomas Jefferson sold his collection to the United States Congress in 1815, it boasted 6,487 titles. Mark Dimunation, chief of the Library of Congress Rare Book and Special Collections Division has stated, "This was the collection that had nursed the Declaration of Independence, that had guided early American diplomacy, that had fueled innovations in American technology, and that assisted a Virginia planter. And now [with Congress's purchase of Jefferson's books in 1815] this collection, built around Jefferson's notion of universal knowledge, was to serve as the source of inspiration and ideas for the new republic" (Fineberg 2008). Books, ideas, and knowledge served to create a future nation. Leaders are readers. They use information to organize and make sense out of what has occurred, why it occurred, and how to create a better future. By using the concepts of memory, reason, and imagination leaders can organize knowledge about the future to move programs and practices into the future.

## VALUE OF HISTORY

Leaders begin by valuing memory or history. Using the history of the profession does not give leaders the right to retreat to comfort zones or the familiarity of how it used to be. Though memory provides knowledge of what used to be, it also is a clear reminder that change is continuous. Leaders understand that change is ongoing.

As Thomas Jefferson used memory to help organize his library, school librarians who are leaders use memory to understand that the rich history of school libraries is not a guarantee of future success. History includes concepts and professional guidance that can be built upon as school librarians journey to the future. Leaders think differently than other people, especially about how decisions are made on the journey through the flood of new ideas and technologies.

## VALUE OF REASON

Reason guides leaders as they propose changes because they understand that even the most sophisticated roadway has bends and turns. They know that the most direct course between two points is a straight line, but wise leaders acknowledge and use the bends and turns to adjust speed and direction. Knowing when to slow down with initiatives and when to accelerate out of the curves provides proper timing for launching new library initiatives.

Leaders value memory because it provides knowledge, and they use reason to provide meaning to changes. Reasoning enables flexibility to adapt strategies and techniques to accomplish change.

## VALUE OF IMAGINATION

As librarians we know the value and impact of a good story. Leaders use stories and analogies to communicate change. They know that effective stories need to be simple and memorable. In addition, leaders express their visions for change through stories. They repeat the concepts often and in different ways because authentic change requires ten times more work and communication than maintaining the status quo.

Leaders use every forum, every speech, and every venue to communicate vision to those in the organization. If memory provides knowledge and reason provides meaning, then imagination shapes the future.

Leaders do not have the benefit of a crystal ball to determine the impact on our profession of future technologies, methodologies, policies, and learning initiatives. But even without a crystal ball, imagination allows leaders to create a vision for moving forward. Imagination also requires leaders to communicate vision in a creative, authentic, clear style. Imagination inspires leaders to cope, maneuver through, and succeed in anticipating the future.

## ESSENTIAL QUALITIES

Using Thomas Jefferson's organizational plan for knowledge to understand the future is a starting point for leadership of change. The next step for leaders is developing three essential qualities. A visionary leader uses integrity, collaboration, and ingenuity when instituting change. School librarians understand that new material and equipment formats, user expectations, and access to information evolve over time. As school librarians research and plan for the future, integrity, collaboration, and imagination become filters for decision making.

### Integrity

Integrity means staying true to library values as listed in the Code of Ethics of the American Library Association. Collaboration requires working with others and bringing in experts to guide and inspire change. Ingenuity involves creative brainstorming to solve problems. Knowing past professional practices and applying professional values to new ideas creates an effective strategy to encourage reform.

Integrity is a leadership trait that guides organizations through uncertain times. Integrity is a stabilizer for organizations. In the field of librarianship integrity is a foundational professional belief. The Code of Ethics of the American Library Association identifies eight areas defining principles of library service. Among the eight values are intellectual freedom, intellectual property rights, and privacy (ALA 2008).

As new formats evolve, issues related to intellectual freedom, intellectual property, privacy, and the First Amendment surface. Librarians who are leaders draw from their professional organizations' literature and expertise for guidance. Ethical issues are not new for librarians because they are confronted with questions related to intellectual freedom, property rights, and privacy whenever new formats are created.

In the past, librarians benefitted from reading editorial reviews of materials and library users benefitted from materials from authoritative sources—

until the Internet came along. Now social-networking sites, blogs, and an immense volume of invalid information are available to anyone with a smart-phone, tablet device, or computer. What leaders do in changing situations is anticipate questions that will be asked. They begin by creating policies and procedures to address those questions.

Using e-books as an example of changing formats; some librarians may jump into buying e-books for their school libraries without considering the consequences. Wise librarian leaders begin by planning ahead, by constructing policies and procedures to guide use of devices and materials in new formats. They consider technology issues as they relate to ensuring that age appropriate e-books are available to students. Now that e-books can be downloaded onto student-owned devices or student-issued computers, school librarians need to configure download processes based on students' interests, needs, and ages.

Authentication measures must be in place prior to an e-book launch be-cause downloading materials takes place at any time and often without the benefit of a librarian who oversees the selection and checkout. Librarians who are leaders build user-authentication into the design of the e-book platform, resulting in selection and material guidance for each student.

When new formats are introduced, leaders are models for best practice. They are honest and reliable when faced with new technology and ideas. Leaders move forward by encouraging ethical use when implementing new policies and practices.

## Collaboration

Collaboration is essential to understanding how colleagues interpret future practices. Leaders know that multiple views and experiences must be dis-cussed when initiating change. For example, if a project is going to involve technology, then leaders know they must collaborate, and include technology advisors and personnel in discussions. Leaders prepare for the future by listen-ing and discussing issues. When leaders collaborate they gain understanding and acceptance by connecting initiatives to the stakeholders' values and vision to gain understanding and acceptance.

Leaders know that stakeholders have common underlying beliefs that create a starting point for exploring change. AASL's *Standards for the 21st-Century Learner* are based on nine common beliefs. These are starting points for librarians to collaborate with teachers and initiate change. Teachers will agree that reading is important, inquiry is a needed framework for learning, ethical behavior is essential for research, technology skills are crucial, equitable access a priority, multiple literacies are making information literacy more complex, learning has a social context, and that school libraries are critical for student learning (AASL 2007).

School librarians are leaders when they use these common beliefs as a starting point for a collaborative dialog aimed at creating future lessons and program access for students. Leaders also know whether new ideas are going to pose an ethical issue, a rights issue, a practical issue, or a power issue before starting collaboration. By understanding and identifying underlying barriers that may create obstacles to collaboration, leaders prevent impediments to change. Collaboration reveals differences and commonalities of user views and needs. Collaborative leadership assists in creating acceptance of future changes to programs and practices.

## Imagination

Leaders who are innovators make creative and inventive choices when solving problems. They anticipate that problems will arise when a process changes. For example, new technologies impact how the policies and procedures in an organization function. In the education field, national and state mandates drive instruction. These are often created in the legislature and, though well-meaning, do not always make sense for implementation at the building level. Librarians who are leaders take those mandates and insert the library program into the process of achieving the mandated goals.

Recently, the state of Virginia changed the evaluation process for teachers and all school personnel, including librarians. One of the key changes was that librarians now need to prove that they positively impact individual student achievement. Anticipating future changes to the evaluation plan, I created an assessment process with the assistance of colleagues and librarians. In my district, the evaluation of school librarians is designed to assess students' mastery and growth in learning as they relate to AASL's *Standards for the 21st-Century Learner*.

Using a state mandate to ensure that librarians were measuring the competencies outlined by the national professional association for school librarians changed instruction for the better. The assessment provides evidence that librarians and library programs are essential to individual student's academic growth.

## KEEPING CURRENT, LOOKING BACK, AND PLANNING AHEAD

Librarians who are leaders stay current on the newest guidelines and standards of the profession and implement them fully. The American Association of School Librarians' strategic plan incorporates research related to changes in the educational profession as the research correlates to school librarians. AASL then creates action plans to address needs surrounding school library programs. The professional organization faces new initiatives with innovative solutions for school librarians. Leaders know that ingenuity solves problems that evolve from change. Librarians who stay current with emerging tools and documents emanating from their professional organizations' research are aware of issues and solutions needed to move their school library programs into the future. Implementing measures suggested by their professional organization is a first step in understanding the future for their library program.

Leaders study the history of their profession because the past is part of organizational memory. They understand the foundational basis for their profession because it is the reason for their existence. Memory and reason provide knowledge and understanding, but innovation is what propels leaders into the future. Librarians who study the history and reason behind changes to library processes and instructional mandates, and then use ingenuity when forming decisions, creating instruction, and initiating change to the library program are exhibiting leadership.

School librarians understand the importance of leadership to the future to their profession. Leaders realize the foundation of effective leadership is professional integrity, the ability to collaborate, and the desire to be innovative. Librarians who develop a vision of the future, while guided by integrity, collaboration, and innovation, guarantee that library programs will remain effective, essential, and relevant.

## LEADERSHIP TIPS RELATED TO UNDERSTANDING THE FUTURE

▶ Understand that every moment is the most important moment because waiting until tomorrow to change is too late.

▶ Provide insight on how to move forward by reflecting and analyzing the past.

▶ Be a visionary leader; for school library programs to survive, all librarians must combine time-tested values of the profession with passion for innovation.

▶ Recognize that reasoning enables flexibility to adapt strategies and techniques to accomplish change.

▶ Read and use your new knowledge to organize and make sense out of what has occurred, why it occurred, and how to create a better future.

▶ Use your imagination, which is essential to creating a vision for moving forward.

▶ Use integrity, collaboration, and ingenuity to confront changes to material and equipment formats, user expectations, and access to information.

▶ Remember that integrity is a foundational belief in the field of librarianship.

▶ Collaborate to connect initiatives with stakeholders' values and vision; as a result, those initiatives will gain understanding and acceptance.

▶ Value the fact that collaboration causes differences and commonalities of user views and needs to surface.

▶ Be an innovator; make creative and inventive choices when solving problems.

# Conclusion

Leadership and librarianship go hand in hand. So many of the skills and dispositions needed to be an effective leader are the very same skills librarians employ to ensure their students are successful. By working together, sharing strategies, and reflecting on personal successes librarians will lead educational initiatives and school library programs into the future. It is this recognition and promotion of leadership principles by school librarians that is helping our students becoming 21st century leaders.

# Works Cited

American Association of School Librarians. 2007. "Standards for the 21st-Century Learner." <www.ala.org/aasl/sites/ala.org.aasl/files/content/guidelinesandstandards/learningstandards/AASL_Learning_Standards_2007.pdf> (accessed March 1, 2013).

———. 2008. "L4L: Learning for Life." <www.ala.org/aasl/sites/ala.org.aasl/files/content/guidelinesandstandards/learning4life/document/l4lplan.pdf> (accessed October 21, 2012).

———. 2009. *Empowering Learners: Guidelines for School Library Programs.* Chicago: ALA.

———. 2013. "L4L Resources." <www.ala.org/aasl/learning4life/resources> (accessed March 1, 2013).

American Association of School Librarians and Association for Educational Communications and Technology. 1998. *Information Power: Building Partnerships for Learning.* Chicago: ALA.

American Library Association. 2008. "Code of Ethics of the American Library Association." <www.ala.org/advocacy/proethics/codeofethics/codeethics> (accessed December 31, 2012).

Ang, Swee Hoon, Siew Meng Leong, and Wendy Yeo. 1999. "When Silence Is Golden: Effects of Silence on Consumer Ad Response." *Advances In Consumer Research* 26: 295–99. <www.acrwebsite.org/search/view-conference-proceedings.aspx?Id=8265> (accessed March 12, 2013).

Associated Press. 2012. "Iranian News Agency Picks Up Onion Article as Fact." *Richmond Times-Dispatch* (September 29). <www2.timesdispatch.com/news/2012/sep/29/iranian-news-agency-picks-onion-article-fact-ar-2244546> (accessed September 30, 2012).

Berka, Justin. 2008. "Apple Wins Eight Design Awards at CeBIT." *Ars Technica* (March 10). <http://arstechnica.com/apple/2008/03/apple-wins-eight-product-design-awards-at-cebit> (accessed September 1, 2012).

BlessingWhite, Inc. 2007. *Innovate on the Run: The Competing Demands of Modern Leadership.* <www.blessingwhite.com/content/reports/Innovate_on_the_Run_NA.pdf> (accessed December 30, 2012).

Bolman, Lee G., and Terrence E. Deal. 2008. *Reframing Organizations: Artistry, Choice, and Leadership,* 4th ed. San Francisco, CA: Jossey-Bass. Kindle Edition.

Bos, Ben. 2011. "Revisiting Schiphol: Benno Wissing and the Airport that Changed the World." *Print* 65 (4): 60–64.

Branyon, Angie. 2013. Interview with the author. January 10.

Bromley, Howard R., and Victoria A. Kirschner-Bromley. 2007. "Are You a Transformational Leader?" *Physician Executive* 33 (6): 54–57.

Carr, Nicholas. 2010. *The Shallows: What the Internet is Doing to Our Brains,* New York: W.W. Norton &Company. Kindle Edition.

Castle Rock Entertainment. 1998. "Seinfeld: The Pitch." <www.sonypictures.com/tv/shows/seinfeld/episode_guide/?sl=episode&ep=403> (accessed October 6, 2012).

CBS Interactive. 2010. "UCLA's Legendary Former Basketball Coach John Wooden Passes Away: National Icon Led Bruins to Multiple NCAA

Titles." <www.uclabruins.com/sports/m-baskbl/spec-rel/060410aae. html> (accessed August 17, 2012).

Collins, Jim. 2001. *Good to Great: Why Some Companies Make the Leap and Others Don't*. New York: HarperCollins.

Colorado Department of Education. 2011. "Introduction to Evidence-Based Practice." *Fast Facts*, November. <www.cde.state.co.us/cdesped/ download/pdf/FF-EBP_MH_Intro.pdf> (accessed January 5, 2013).

Cooper, Anderson. 2012. "Michael Phelps: Ready for London Games." <www.cbsnews.com/8301-18560_162-57476222/michael-phelps-ready-for-london-games> (accessed March 18, 2013).

Cooper, Robert K. 2001. *The Other 90%: How to Unlock Your Vast Untapped Potential for Leadership and Life*. New York: Three Rivers.

———. 2006. *Get Out of Your Own Way: The 5 Keys to Surpassing Everyone's Expectations*. New York: Crown Business.

da Vinci, Leonardo. 2012. "Time Stays Long Enough." BrainyQuote. <www.brainyquote.com/quotes/quotes/l/leonardoda379160.html> (accessed August 24, 2012).

Davis, Brooke, and Virginia Brown. 2012. Interview with the author. September 10.

Dictionary.com. 2012. "Groupthink." <http://dictionary.reference.com/ browse/groupthink> (accessed September 16, 2012).

DiMattia, Susan. 2005. "Silence Is Olden." *American Libraries* 36 (1): 48–51.

Dorausch, Michael. 2009. "Chiropractor Talks about 2009 Belmont Stakes." *Chiropractic Blogs* (June 6). <http://blog.planetc1.com/ chiropractor-talks-about-2009-belmont-stakes> (accessed October 7, 2012).

Dougherty, Tom. 2010. "How Coke Lost its Fizz—and Other Branding Lessons." <www.stealingshare.com/pages/Coke%20Branding%20 Lessons.htm> (accessed September 15, 2012).

Einstein, Albert. 2009. "The CAE Guy." <www.nafems.org/caeguy/apr09> (accessed March 16, 2013).

Emerson, Ralph Waldo. 2013. "Well Done Quotes." <www.brainyquote. com/quotes/keywords/well_done.html> (accessed March 16, 2013).

Encyclopaedia Britannica. 2013. "Tropical Cyclone." <www.britannica.
com/EBchecked/topic/606551/tropical-cyclone> (accessed October 06,
2012).

Fagan, Ryan. "Powering Up For London: Michael Phelps Is Back but
Will New Approach Cost Him Gold?" <http://aol.sportingnews.com/
olympics/story/2012-05-31/london-2012-summer-olympics-michael-
phelps-training-gold-medals-beijing> (accessed July 28, 2012).

Farlex, Inc. 2012a. "Reflection." *The Free Dictionary*. <www.
thefreedictionary.com/reflection> (accessed December 5, 2012).

———. 2012b. "Status Quo." *The Free Dictionary*. <www.thefreedictionary.
com/status+quo> (accessed December 5, 2012).

Fetscher, Suzanne. 2008. "Innovative Cultures." *Leadership Excellence* 25 (4):
17.

Fineberg, Gail. 2008. "Thomas Jefferson's Library: Library Reconstructs,
Displays Founding Collection." *Library of Congress Information
Bulletin* (June). <www.loc.gov/loc/lcib/0806/jefferson.html> (accessed
December 31, 2012).

Fitzpatrick, Frank, and Zach Tuckwiller. 2012. "The Third Annual Longdale
Elementary Pig Race." <http://vimeo.com/41369945> (accessed August
26, 2012).

Gilpatrick, Kristin. 2001. "Lessons Learned...In Negotiation." *Credit Union
Management* 24 (6): 16.

Goldsmith, Marshall, and Patricia Wheeler. 2007. "Leaders as Coaches."
*Leadership Excellence* 24 (8): 6–7. <www.marshallgoldsmithlibrary.com/
cim/articles_display.php?aid=656> (accessed March16, 2013).

Goodreads Inc. 2013. "Quotes about Status Quo." <www.goodreads.com/
quotes/tag/status-quo> (accessed March 12, 2013).

Graham, Billy. 2012. "Billy Graham Quotes." SearchQuotes. <www.
searchquotes.com/quotation/A_keen_sense_of_humor_helps_us_
to_overlook_the_unbecoming,_understand_the_unconventional,_
tolerated_/239880> (accessed August 26, 2012).

Hally, Nancy. 2012. Interview with the author. September 10.

Harry S. Truman Library and Museum. n.d. "'The Buck Stops Here' Desk
Sign." <www.trumanlibrary.org/buckstop.htm> (accessed October 30,
2012).

Hawkins, Joseph A. 2000. "To Upend the Status Quo." *Education Week* 19 (30): 39.

Ho, Li-Hsing, et al. "Influence of Humorous Leadership at Workplace on the Innovative Behavior of Leaders and Their Leadership Effectiveness" *African Journal of Business Management* 5 (16): 6674–83. <http://researcher.nsc.gov.tw/public/chcjyh/Data/11261544171.pdf> (accessed August 26, 2012).

Holland, David. 2012. "Marie Kelleher Breaks Barrier: Richmonder Sets 2 National Records in 100–104 Age Group." <www.vaswim.org/2012/05/marie-kelleher-breaks-barrier> (accessed July 28, 2012).

Homsey, Harvey H. H. 2010. "Mentor or Protegé? A Formal Mentorship Program is the Answer." *Franchising World* 42 (1): 104. <www.franchise.org/Franchise-Industry-News-Detail.aspx?id=48762#> (accessed March 18, 2013).

Howard, Maria. 2012. "Fitness: Virginia Senior Games." *Richmond-Times Dispatch* (May 6). <www2.timesdispatch.com/lifestyles/2012/may/06/tdflair04-fitness-virginia-senior-games-ar-1886339> (accessed August 24, 2012).

Howe, Desson. 1994. "True Lies." *Washington Post* (July 15). <www.washingtonpost.com/wp-srv/style/longterm/movies/videos/trueliesrhowe_a0b075.htm> (accessed September 15, 2012).

Howe, Susan, and Margaret Marquis. 2012. Interview with the author. September 10.

Idaho State Police. 2011. "'Stop Speeding before It Stops You' Campaign." *Idaho State Police News and Information Blog* (April 6). <http://idahostatepolice.blogspot.com/2011/04/stop-speeding-before-it-stops-you_06.html> (accessed September 15, 2012).

Jackson, John Bradley. 2006. "Silence and Negotiation." <http://ezinearticles.com/?Silence-and-Negotiation&id=394167> (accessed October 6, 2012).

Jankowski, Amy, and Talitha Matlin. 2012. "Going on Reference Safari: Bringing the Library to Zookeepers and Horticulturists in their Native Habitat." Poster session presented at American Library Association Annual Conference. June 21–26. Anaheim, CA.

Jenks, Andy. 2009. "Shooting at high school in Henrico; One student in custody." <www.nbc12.com/Global/story.asp?S=11141961&Call=Email&Format=HTML> (accessed March 26, 2013).

Jones, Jami L. "Caring: A Bridge to a New Era." *Knowledge Quest* 40 (5): 6–7.

Keep, William W. 2012. "The Worrisome Ascendance of Business in Higher Education." *Chronicle of Higher Education* (June 21). <http://chronicle.com/article/The-Worrisome-Ascendance-of/132501> (accessed June 30, 2012).

Kerfoot, Karlene M. "On Leadership. Direct Decision Making vs. Oblique Decision Making: Which Is Right?" *Nursing Economic$* 29 (5): 290–91.

Knapp, Michael S., Michael A. Copland, and Joan E. Talbert. 2003. "Leading for Learning: Reflective Tools for School and District Leaders." Seattle: Center for the Study of Teaching and Policy, University of Washington. <http://depts.washington.edu/ctpmail/PDFs/LforLSummary-02-03.pdf> (accessed March 17, 2013).

Lombardi, Vince, Jr. 2002. *The Lombardi Rules: 26 Lessons from Vince Lombardi—The World's Greatest Coach*. New York: McGraw-Hill. Kindle Edition.

Martin, Charlie. 2012. Interview with the author. August 27.

Mason, Mark. 2007. "Critical Thinking and Learning." *Educational Philosophy and Theory* 39 (4): 339–49.

McKelway, Bill. 2013. "Ten Years Later, Sniper Saga Still Defies Comprehension." *Richmond-Times Dispatch* (January 17). <www.timesdispatch.com/news/ten-years-later-sniper-saga-still-defies-comprehension/article_2075720e-07c7-5635-af50-9034ad9dc9b4.html> (accessed March 18, 2013).

Mills, Melinda F. 2012. Interview with the author. October 12.

Morgan, Elizabeth A. 2012. Interview with the author. August 17.

National Oceanic and Atmospheric Administration, National Climatic Data Center. 2005. "Hurricane Katrina." <www.ncdc.noaa.gov/special-reports/katrina.html> (accessed September 3, 2012).

Newman, Delia. 2012. "Information is the Building Block for Learning." *Knowledge Quest* 40 (3): 24–28.

Newman, Rick. 2011. "Where Steve Jobs Ranks among the Greats." *U.S. News and World Report* (October 6). <www.usnews.com/news/blogs/rick-newman/2011/10/06/where-steve-jobs-ranks-among-the-greats> (accessed March 18, 2013).

Noddings, Nel. 1995. "Teaching Themes of Caring." *Education Digest* 61 (3): 24–28.

Cavallaro, Gina, interviewed by Michele Norris. 2006. "Not Just Strong, Army Strong." <www.npr.org/templates/story/story.php?storyId=6256042> (accessed September 15, 2012).

Phillips, Donald T. 1992. *Lincoln on Leadership: Executive Strategies for Tough Times.* New York: Warner.

Pink, Daniel H. 2009. *Drive: The Surprising Truth about What Motivates Us.* New York: Riverhead Books.

Powell, Colin. 2012. *It Worked For Me: In Life and Leadership.* New York: Harper.

R. R. Bowker. 1998. "Truman, Harry S. (1884–1972)." *From Biography To History. Biography Reference Center.*

Ragland, Vicki. 2012. Interview with the author. September 10.

Rix, Kate. 2012. "Are Librarians Still Important?" *Scholastic Administr@ tor.* <www.scholastic.com/browse/article.jsp?id=3757441> (accessed October 21, 2012).

Roberts, Kathleen. 2012. Interview with the author. September 12.

Rouse, Margaret. 2012. "Infographics." <http://whatis.techtarget.com/definition/infographics> (accessed September 30, 2012).

Safi, Asila, and Darrell Norman Burrell. "Developing Advanced Decision-Making Skills in International Leaders and Managers." *Vikalpa: The Journal for Decision Makers* 32 (3):1–8. <http://drhornsby.com/uop/MBA%20521/week%203/safi.pdf> (accessed March 16, 2013).

Salbach, Nancy M., and Susan B. Jaglal. 2011. "Creation and Validation of the Evidence-Based Practice Confidence Scale for Health Care Professionals." *Journal of Evaluation in Clinical Practice* 17 (4): 794–800.

Schardt, Connie, and Jill Mayer. 2010. "What is Evidence Based Practice (EBP)?" <www.hsl.unc.edu/services/tutorials/ebm/whatis.htm> (accessed January 2, 2013).

Schmoker, Mike. 1994. "Unlocking the Potential for Success." *Oregonian* (January 9) D1+.

Schneider, Brendan. 2013. "HOWTO: Start using Twitter for Your School" <www.schneiderb.com/howto-start-using-twitter-for-your-school> (accessed March 28, 2013).

Schudel, Mark. 2006. "Henriette Avram, Mother of MARC, Dies." *Library of Congress Information Bulletin* (May). <www.loc.gov/loc/lcib/0605/avram.html> (accessed December 30, 2012).

Simon, Paul. 2012. "Sounds of Silence Lyrics." <www.metrolyrics.com/sounds-of-silence-lyrics-paul-simon.html> (accessed October 13, 2012).

Simpllico, Joseph. 2002. "Miscommunication in the Classroom: What Teachers Say and What Students Really Hear." *Education* 122 (3): 599–601.

Snyder, Steven. 2012. "The Lincoln-Stevens Debate: Your True North and the Swamp." <www.snyderleadership.com/2012/11/18/the-lincoln-stevens-debate-your-true-north-and-the-swamp> (accessed December 3, 2012).

Spector, Bertram I. 1996, "Metaphors of International Negotiation." *International Negotiation* 1 (1): 1–9.

Sports Publications International. 2012. "Streamlined News, Dec. 21." <www.swimmingworldmagazine.com/lane9/news/MorningSwimShow/32987.asp> (accessed March 2, 2013).

Srivastava, Abhishek, Kathryn M. Bartol, and Edwin A. Locke. 2006. "Empowering Leadership in Management Teams: Effects on Knowledge Sharing, Efficacy, and Performance." *Academy of Management Journal* 49 (6): 1239–51.

Stahl, Dulcelina. 1998. "Manage, Lead, Inspire." *Nursing Management* 29 (10):18–21.

Summitt, Pat, with Sally Jenkins. 1999. *Reach for the Summit: The Definite Dozen System for Succeeding at Whatever You Do*. New York: Broadway Books.

Szalavitz, Maia. 2011. "Why Laughing at Yourself May be Good for You: First Ever Study." *Time* (August 9). <http://healthland.time.

com/2011/08/09/why-laughing-at-yourself-may-be-good-for-you-first-ever-study> (accessed August 26, 2012).

Tague, Nancy R. 2004. *The Quality Toolbox*, 2nd ed. Milwaukee, WI: ASQ Quality Press, 247–49. <http://asq.org/learn-about-quality/cause-analysis-tools/overview/fishbone.html> (accessed March 16, 2013).

"Taking a Proactive Stance." 1996. *Chain Store Age* 72 (8): 14E.

"Ted Turner." 2011. *Columbia Electronic Encyclopedia*, 6th ed. New York: Columbia University Press.

Todd, Ross. "The Evidence-Based Manifesto." *School Library Journal* 54 (4): 38–43.

U.S. Department of Defense. 2011. DoD 5500.007-R, Section 4, Ethical Values. <www.dtic.mil/whs/directives/corres/pdf/550007r.pdf> (accessed September 3, 2012).

U.S. Marine Corps. 2012. "Principles & Values." <www.marines.com/history-heritage/principles-values> (accessed September 15, 2012).

Unger, Mike. 2012. "Phelps Out of Water." *Baltimore* (July). <www.baltimoremagazine.net/features/2012/07/michael-phelps-out-of-water-2012-olympics> (accessed August 3, 2012).

Wade, Jon, ed. 2012. "Michael Phelps—Greatest Olympic Swimmer—Workouts and Diet." <www.motleyhealth.com/news/michael-phelps-greatest-olympic-swimmer-workouts-and-diet> (accessed August 3, 2012).

Webb, Brandon, with John David Mann. 2012. *The Red Circle: My Life in the Navy SEAL Sniper Corps and How I Trained America's Deadliest Marksman*. New York: St. Martin's Press.

Wenner, Kathryn S. 2002. "Peeling the Onion." *American Journalism Review* (September). <www.ajr.org/Article.asp?id=2618> (accessed September 30, 2012).

Whiteside, Kelly. 2012. "Mike Krzyzewski for His Country: 'The Ultimate Honor'." *USA Today* (July 20). <http://usatoday30.usatoday.com/sports/olympics/london/basketball/story/2012-07-18/Mike-Krzyzewski-Olympic-basketball/56344940/1> (accessed March 18, 2013).

Wiersma, Uco J. 1992. "The Effects of Extrinsic Rewards in Intrinsic Motivation: A Meta-Analysis." *Journal of Occupational and Organizational Psychology* 65 (2): 101–114.

Winter, Michael. 2012. "UVa President Teresa Sullivan Reinstated." *USA Today* (June 26). <http://content.usatoday.com/communities/ondeadline/post/2012/06/uva-president-teresa-sullivan-reinstated/1> (accessed September 16, 2012).

# Appendix A
## Index

# Appendix B

## Learning4Life (L4L)

### A National Plan for Implementation of
*Standards for the 21st-Century Learner*
**and** *Empowering Learners: Guidelines
for School Library Programs*

An initiative of the American Association of School Librarians

This implementation plan was created to support states, school systems, and individual schools preparing to implement the *Standards for the 21st-Century Learner* and *Empowering Learners: Guidelines for School Library Programs.* The plan will also increase awareness and understanding of the learning standards and program guidelines and create a committed group of stakeholders with a shared voice.

While the standards and guidelines define what "should be" in terms of information literacy, research through guided inquiry, and the integration of technology in the traditional school context, they also acknowledge varied and new forms of teaching and learning in a social and global context. Foundational to this plan is the fundamental value of reading, core content, and mastery of skills that produce deep knowledge and understanding, as well as the portable skills that serve individuals for a lifetime, making them critical thinkers, problem solvers, and continually evolving learners.

To this end, the implementation plan addresses the practical realization of these important skills and values as it:

- identifies guiding principles and an overarching position and branding statement;
- identifies target audiences (internal and external);
- identifies training opportunities and resources;
- provides a communication plan;
- provides a plan for continuous feedback, evaluation, and sustainability;
- provides a plan for endorsements and support;
- provides supporting documents.

The plan is available online at <www.ala.org/aasl/learning4life>.

Interlocking Pieces Graphic designed
by Louis Henry Mitchell

# Appendix C

## Learning4Life Publications

*Available from the American Association
of School Librarians*

Learning4Life (L4L): A National Plan for
Implementation of *Standards for the 21st-Century
Learner* and *Empowering Learners: Guidelines for
School Library Programs*

> Available for download at <www.ala.org/aasl/
> learning4life>.

*Standards for the 21st-Century Learner* (2007)

> Available for download from the AASL Web
> site. Packets of full-color brochures may also be
> purchased. Visit <www.ala.org/aasl/standards>.

*Standards for the 21st-Century Learner in Action*
(2009)

> Available for purchase at <www.ala.org/aasl/
> standardsinaction>.

*Empowering Learners: Guidelines for School Library
Programs* (2009)

> Available for purchase at <www.ala.org/aasl/
> guidelines>.

*A Planning Guide for Empowering Learners with School Library Program Assessment Rubric* (2010)

> Available for purchase at <www.aasl.eb.com>, or for more information and resources visit <www.ala.org/aasl/planningguide>.

*A 21st-Century Approach to School Librarian Evaluation* (2012)

> Available for purchase at <www.ala.org/aasl/evaluationworkbook>.

*Library Spaces for 21st-Century Learners: A Planning Guide for Creating New School Library Concepts* (2013)

> Available for purchase at <www.ala.org/aasl/libraryspaces>.

*Empowering Leadership: Developing Behaviors for Success* (2013)

> Available for purchase at <www.ala.org/aasl/leadership>.